from hopeless
TO VICTORIOUS

By
Shalil Forrest

MAPLE
PUBLISHERS

from hopeless TO VICTORIOUS

Author: Shalil Forrest

Copyright © Shalil Forrest (2025)

The right of Shalil Forrest to be identified as author of this work has been asserted by the author in accordance with section 77 and 78 of the Copyright, Designs and Patents Act 1988.

First Published in 2025

ISBN 978-1-83538-628-6 (Hardback)
     978-1-83538-629-3 (E-Book)

Book cover design and layout by:
     Maple Publishers
     www.maplepublishers.com

Published by:
     Maple Publishers
     Fairbourne Drive, Atterbury,
     Milton Keynes,
     MK10 9RG, UK
     www.maplepublishers.com

A CIP catalogue record for this title is available from the British Library.

All rights reserved. No part of this book may be reproduced or translated by any form or by any means, electronic or mechanical, including photocopying, recording or by any information storage and retrieval system without written permission from the author.

The book is a work of fiction. Unless otherwise indicated, all the names, characters, places and incidents are either the product of the author's imagination or used in a fictitious manner. Any resemblance to actual people living or dead, events or locales is entirely coincidental, and the Publisher hereby disclaims any responsibility for them.

CONTENTS

Chapter 1 – Custody/Visitation 4

Chapter 2 – My Battle with Depression/ Winning the battle Within me ... 33

Chapter 3 – (Abortion) Shedding of Innocent Blood (2015) 38

Chapter 4 – What Happens when you didn't ask for the calling on your life to be A Prophetess called to the Nations 42

Chapter 5 – Forgiving Myself and others.. 46

Chapter 6 – Witchcraft (Spiritual Wickedness in High Places) 48

Chapter 7 – I was afflicted -he healed my body 60

Chapter 8 – My Knight and Shining Armor... 61

Chapter 9 – Miscarriage 65

Chapter 1
Custody/Visitation

For many years, I remember going through an ongoing and very nasty custody battle. Nothing or no one could have ever prepared me for what I was about to go through emotionally, mentally and spiritually. I should have known what I was in for to some degree because when I was pregnant, out of anger he told me to get an ABORTION. I ignored that and just tried to remain strong and healthy for the sake of our baby girl that was growing inside of me. I can remember her father and I getting into an argument about her name. I can admit that we were both stubborn on the topic of her name. I was set on what I wanted to name her and he was set on what he wanted to name her. I don't know why but I loved "Niya" and wanted her name to have "Niya" in it. I was okay with her having his last name and even the beginning of her name having the same first initial of his name.

I can remember us getting into this big argument and it even began to involve some of our family members all because of a name. He wanted her name to be Sydney which I didn't hate but I also didn't want that to be her name because there was this man by that name that creeped me out that worked in the same building as me and I expressed this to him. Emotions were very high and I couldn't believe the reality of what I was getting/had gotten myself into. I really didn't know much about the importance of being equally yoked and really being on one accord with someone as your partner. Boy was I in for a rude awakening. If someone would have told me beforehand it still probably couldn't have prepared me for what I had gotten myself into. I can remember when we met it was a few days after my birthday February 15th in 2009 as I was on my way to work passing by Zoom's (a convenience store) which is now 7 Eleven.

I was open to talking to someone new but I now realize I wasn't healed from my past and neither was he based on the conversations we had. Much like other women unknowingly I felt at the time, like I could be the difference in his life and the person that could help him "heal." I had to realize and come to the understanding that without giving myself the proper time to heal I made decisions based off of my feelings and definitely misguided judgment. To add insult to injury, I was 19 years old. I can remember one of our first conversations and he told me how some of the females from his previous relationships did this and that to him and in my mind not really knowing him that well, he really had me convinced. I just wanted to be that girl that would change the narrative of how the story was previously going for him and be someone who could "help him trust and love again."

I quickly realized I wasn't completely over my ex so this was like a rebound relationship for me that moved much faster than I could have ever prepared myself for. When we first met, I didn't see it but I had so many red flags but I was too blind to see. Sometimes we can't see clearly when we are in something or maybe we refuse to see until we have no choice but to see. I definitely didn't follow the "90-day rule." He was passionate in the bedroom and was a pleaser. I can remember our first time he cut on some r&b and anyone who knows me knows that music is my love language. I can remember feeling in love in that moment but also after thinking what had I just gotten myself into. Yes, we used protection the first few times. I can remember calling who I often referred to as my twin cousin and sharing what had just happened and she told me about her day and night as well. I can remember saying: "Girl, OMG what did I just do? It was not supposed to happen that soon as it had only been a few weeks. She laughed and told me girl you're fine, it happens. We continued to talk and laugh about our good memories from childhood and our plans for the future.

For some reason or another I stopped using protection and thought I couldn't get pregnant. We continued to date, have fun and do what "young adults" did. I can remember preparing for Black Bike Week in Myrtle Beach, SC that year and I was excited as I was going with my older sisters, some of my cousins and some of our mutual friends. We went and had a ball. I was never much of a drinker and still to date I have never smoked in my life. In Myrtle

Beach this particular year, I did have a few drinks and can remember being on the phone with him and him telling me how he was going to get me pregnant when I came back from Myrtle Beach. I was like oh nah I don't think so and said to myself I need to get on birth control as soon as I get back home because AHT AHT that was not a part of the plan.

Well to my surprise when I got back to Virginia, I started feeling sick and noticed that I had missed my cycle. I can remember telling him and being scared because I was nervous for myself and I wasn't sure what he was going to say. To my surprise he was a lot more excited than he should have been because umm no this is not supposed to be happening right now, we were still getting to know each other. I was nervous and scared to even go get a pregnancy test because so much was running through my head. My sister convinced me to go to the good ole dollar tree and get a test so that's exactly what I did. I came back home and I took the test and couldn't believe my eyes. It was showing that I was in fact pregnant. I had so many emotions and mixed feelings running through my mind but I was very grateful that he seemed to be supportive but I had to face the reality that I was pregnant by a man I barely even knew. We hadn't even really been through anything together. We hadn't planned for this but the reality of it is we didn't plan against it when we stopped using protection.

This day was certainly unlike any other and I was afraid to tell my parents and my two eldest sisters. I can't exactly remember their reactions but they were more encouraging than I expected and let me know that it was a new life and despite how I felt it was not something that I should beat myself up about but to instead accept it and start preparing. At this point in my life I knew of God, but I didn't know God, you gotta catch that. I knew nothing about having a personal relationship with God. I did still feel like a baby was a blessing from God. Like many others, I attended church and that was it. I did have a desire for more just didn't quite know how to get there just yet. Unfortunately our first pregnancy ended in miscarriage and we were hurt but before I could get on birth control I found myself pregnant again.

As the months grew so did my belly and the realization that I was going to be someone's mother. I would have never thought in a million years little ole me would have someone calling me mommy. In fact, I remember saying I didn't want any children as I'm sure many others said prior to being pregnant and it actually becoming a reality for us.

Just like any other relationship we went through many ups and downs which included sharing some laughs and some tears. He was very supportive and made sure that he was at the doctor's appointments and silly things to try to brighten my days but while reminding me how mean I was. He would rub my stomach and talk to our growing baby girl. She knew when he was around because she would start kicking and moving around when she would hear his voice and feel him touching my belly.

Fast forward to February of 2010, it was not only my birthday month but it was also the month of our baby shower. I was grateful that my family and some of my friends took it upon themselves to plan me an amazing baby shower. I can remember the night before staying at one of my older sister's houses and just catching up and bonding with her. It was her job to help me get ready for the baby shower the next day and she was also tasked with doing my makeup.

The baby shower turned out really nice. The food was great of course, my family is like that when it comes to cooking (blessed with the gift of cooking), well most of us lol. We received an abundance of gifts. Our baby girl was really blessed and fully stocked up on clothes and necessities to help get us off to a great start as new parents. We welcomed her into the world the following month. As the time grew closer for me to give birth, I was consumed with emotions about what kind of mommy I would be and how I would balance everything. I prayed often that she would be healthy, strong and of course that she would be a beautiful baby girl.

My initial due date was April 5th but as I grew closer to my due date my doctor pulled me out of work sooner than I was originally scheduled to come out of work. When I went to what would be my last official doctor's appointment before giving birth, I was informed that I had a very mild case of pre-eclampsia. The good news was that I was already considered full term so I didn't have to stress or worry about her being born prematurely and the many complications that can come along with that. However, I also didn't expect that I would get a call later that day from the doctor that I had too much protein in my urine and that I needed to come to the hospital so they could monitor me. After I called and made her father aware of the news, we drove to the hospital together and after just a few hours I was admitted to the hospital because they were going to need to induce my labor.

    They advised me since I was already considered full term and I was still showing as having too much protein in my urine it wasn't beneficial for me to be pregnant any longer. I was shocked, excited and scared all at the same time. They began the process that night which was March 25th about 11pm and March 26th at 5:30 pm I naturally gave birth to a beautiful baby girl who came out looking just like her father. I can remember when I reached 10cms dilated, the nurse came in to check on me for the last time and she had a look of worry on her face. I knew it was about time for me to push and so did she. Unfortunately, it was the time that the doctors were changing shifts or rotation and the doctor that was to deliver our baby was in Friday rush hour traffic. At this point…. I didn't care how or who was going to deliver her, all I knew was somebody better make an executive decision and expeditiously, because she was ready to make her grand entrance and I couldn't resist the urge to push. Thankfully the doctor got there quickly and we had a successful delivery with no complications and she was healthy. She did have to stay at the hospital for a couple extra days due to what is referred to as jaundice or bilirubin. I learned it was a normal thing but to a first-time mom all I knew was my baby had to stay behind and she couldn't leave the hospital when I did. We made sure to be there by her side every step of the way until she was able to come home which I believe was two or three days later. It seemed like forever. She was the sweetest and easiest baby to care for. She was very alert and the most beautiful chocolate baby, she was so special to me. I had to wake her up most of the time to eat because she slept really well which, I wasn't complaining about at all.

    Her father would stay nights to help me after work and just to relieve me because being a first-time mommy wasn't a walk in the park. Again, she was a great baby and pretty easy to deal with but when you take into account trying to physically heal and having postpartum depression, I was grateful to have a good support system to include family and friends.

Let's fast-forward to about a week and a half in. Her father got off of work and while I knew he had just worked a full shift I too was tired and wanted just like 30 mins to an hour to myself to breathe and have a moment. I had no idea this would create an argument and start what would be a long road ahead. NOTHING and I mean NOTHING could have prepared me for what was to come. I can remember telling him if you are not going to help with her then you can just go home tonight, it's really no point for me to watch you sleep. He proceeded and said that he wasn't leaving... I told him yes you are, I think it's best we just need to give each other some space anyway. He told me if he had to leave that she was leaving with him. Of course, I said NO she isn't, she is going to stay here as I wholeheartedly believed it was too early for her to be staying somewhere without me. I just didn't feel right with her leaving with him and we had just gotten into an argument especially because he initially didn't want to relieve me for 30 mins so I could have a few moments to myself. He proceeded to call his mom and pack a baby bag for our daughter. She pleaded with me to just let him take her for the night so I could get some rest. I gave it some thought but I just had a really uneasy feeling about it. I had no one else home with me and I kind of felt outnumbered. Almost immediately after they left, I started receiving text messages from him saying how he was going to keep her and I wasn't going to see her for a long time and he also stated that he was going to take her to Tennessee. Just wrap your head around receiving that type of text message right after your baby left for what you thought was going to be an overnight stay with her father and paternal grandmother.

I felt so dumb and helpless. I began to cry and feel guilty for not standing my ground more and the messages continued to roll in and as much as I wanted to and tried to ignore them, they were very upsetting to me. I reached out to his mom and let her know what was being said to me and she just suggested that I calm down and ignore him as he was just saying those things to get me upset and that he was going to bring her back tomorrow and that he was not going to take her out of town. My dad was out to sea at the time and when my mom walked in the house, I immediately told her what was going on. She tried to calm me down and console me. She tried to reach out to both him and his mother and it didn't turn out too well so we had no choice but to wait until the morning and see how getting her back was going to turn out.

    I called my oldest sister and she came over in the morning and all three of us: my mom, eldest sister and myself proceeded to head over to their house to exchange her back like it was discussed the night prior. When we arrived, we all expected a smooth exchange and this is when I learned that in the State of Virginia that no one legally has custody until you actually petition the courts for custody of YOUR OWN CHILD. One thing about this man he was definitely book smart and he hit me with the "possession is 9/10 of the law" and right now she was in his physical custody so when he refused to voluntarily give her back even with calling the police it was nothing that the police could do. We tried to be as nice and peaceful as possible, my mom pleaded with his mother woman to woman. One of the things I specifically can remember her saying to her is: "you know as a woman and new mom she needs to be home with her mom. His mom's argument was "Well it's his child too and this argument and situation just allowed me to see a side of him that I never knew existed. But then again I didn't know this man…. I just really hoped I would soon wake up from this nightmare cause surely this was not my reality. This situation allowed me to see that he knew from the very moment that he took her what he was doing and he didn't care how it made me feel or how it affected me as her mother.

    It seemed like all he knew was since he couldn't have his way the night before he was going to make me suffer by keeping our daughter. The police came and took a report and confirmed what he already said. Neither one of us had custody so this was not a matter that they could get involved with but they did advise that we go to the juvenile and domestic relations courthouse and petition for custody as soon as possible because until then no one would have custody and it belonged to the state until then. Just them acknowledging there was nothing they could do in that moment was heartbreaking and I felt so defeated and I really couldn't understand why this was happening to me. What did I do to deserve this? This really hurt me to my core and I couldn't stop crying. I was so stressed out and it only made my stomach issues worse because I had IBS which is short for irritable bowel syndrome. Irritable bowel syndrome was most certainly onset and heightened by stress much like many other things that affect our bodies.

The next day he let me know he was going over to his aunt's house and that I could come over and see our daughter. I said "umm what do you mean I can come over and see her, why should I have to come over and see her?" I gathered myself and asked my eldest sister to come with me as I didn't trust anyone from his family at this point. I just needed someone who I knew actually had my best interest at heart at this point, by my side. We went over to his aunt's house where they were. We were invited to come in and I washed my hands so I could hold and embrace my baby girl after what felt like FOREVER. Everything started out okay and the plan was to sit down and create a schedule that we both could agree on at least until we went to court to have a more permanent agreement put in place. Again, things were going well until he got mad because of a comment that was made. I can't for the life of me remember exactly what was said to make him change his mind and snap so abruptly but whatever it was changed the course of everything for the rest of that day. I can remember him saying I'm not agreeing with anything or signing anything, you'll see her again when we go to court. You can just imagine the host of emotions that begin to well up on the inside of me all over again. It was as if I was a yo-yo and he was a kid that was in control of it. We were upstairs in his aunt's room and he went downstairs for something, so remaining in the room was me holding our daughter, my sister, his mom and his aunt. Once his aunt realized that he was being very uncooperative in this situation she told me to go in her bathroom with our baby and she was going to lock her door and call the police so I could have her in my arms when they arrived. He must have quickly gotten wind of what was going on because he came banging on her door demanding to be let in the room and asking his mom if she was a part of this plan. She insisted she wasn't and kept repeating "it wasn't me it wasn't me." Shortly thereafter the police came and my sister said "I'm bigger than you give me the baby because I know he will try to take her out of your hands but it's going to take a little more from him to take her from me." Indeed, she was right. We proceeded to leave the room and head down the stairs. I went ahead of my sister and she came down directly after me. We couldn't even get halfway down the stairs without him trying to take our daughter out of my sister's hands. It was scary to say the least. Here we have our newborn baby in my sister's arms and he was literally trying to pry her out of my sister's arms. As you can imagine things got very heated and scary all at the same time. When I reached the bottom of the stairs, I went to grab her car seat and leave but of course he wasn't having it. Again, this wasn't a matter that police could intervene in, they simply tried to control the situation but they ended up calling CPS on us. He bought the carseat and because he didn't want her to leave with me, he said that we could not take the car seat he bought for OUR CHILD. My sister had to leave to go to Kmart to buy another car seat so we could leave. I now know looking back that it was nothing but the grace of God that even though CPS was called and came out that no further action was taken and our baby wasn't taken away that day.

They said if we couldn't come to a resolution then they would have no choice but to step in so that's when he finally said fine take her but we could not take the car seat that he bought for our daughter. I left grateful and thankful but also mentally and emotionally drained. What was supposed to be one of the happiest times in my life was now beginning to feel like a nightmare that I so desperately wanted to wake up from. My baby girl and I ended up staying at my sister's house which was about 20-30 mins away depending on traffic just so I could clear my head and get away from the immediate area. Her father and I eventually talked I believe a couple of days later and arranged a visitation for him to see her and spend time with her until we went to court. Of course, every time he came around in the beginning after this was extremely uncomfortable and I always wondered if he was going to run off with her and try to overpower me.

I had no idea what was to be expected with court in the custody/visitation matter and when I found out the scope of everything, I wished things weren't the way they were and I wouldn't have wished this on anyone. I also realized with things the way they were and her being so young it was unfortunately a very necessary process. This was all new to me and I just wanted it to be over already just as quick as it was beginning. I didn't know it at the time but this was the beginning of a VERY LONG ROAD of constant back and forth proceedings to court. If you have never had to go through the courts for custody/visitation matters it is my prayer that you never will. I pray that you pay attention to the red flags that we often pray for but ignore when we want to see the good in everyone.

To every young woman or man if no one has ever told you having a child by someone that you are unequally yoked with is not the way or as some say "not it." I love our baby girl as she is a blessing to our lives and everyone she encounters but again NOTHING could have prepared me for what I was dealing with in regards to the back-and-forth court proceedings in Juvenile and Domestic Relations Court for custody and visitation. For starters both parties have to take a parenting class which is not a bad idea but still, maybe this should have been a requirement during pregnancy before the child is born. They assign a court date once the paperwork is filed and the first court date is set where you think you will get a decision or trial that day. If both parents can't agree to an agreement which is usually almost never then you have to go through a mediator and the child is assigned a lawyer which is referred to guardian ad litem who is supposed to represent the best interest of the child.

In this case she was a newborn and unable to speak for herself so it turned into a process where we both had an interview separately with the guardian ad litem. Another court date is set usually several moments later during this time the guardian does her job in these matters. Sometimes, the initial interview is conducted over the phone and based on the visits and interviews, the child's age, the parent's living conditions and a number of other factors a recommendation is made before the courts by the guardian and the judge after hearing testimony from both parents makes the final determination.

We both agreed on joint custody with me having primary physical custody but the visitation is where things started to go bad. He wanted a visitation schedule that was considered liberal visitation whereas I felt it would be best to have something more structured so that it would allow us to know ahead of time when we would have her and it would allow us to plan ahead and accordingly. His argument was that would control or limit his time with her which was not at all the case but more so to keep the peace. I just didn't want to have grey areas as far as visitation that allowed for other problems to creep in or arise because that would mean it wasn't crystal clear when she was supposed to be with which parent.

Our first custody/visitation order put in place required that he gave me 96 hours' notice when he wanted to exercise his visitation. I felt that was a good time as it was not too far in advance but it was also not too short of a notice. He was not happy with the decision as he stated he should not have to give me that much notice to come see or pick up our daughter. In a perfect world we wouldn't have been here and no notice at all would have been required but here we were.

This was shortly before I got my first apartment and moved to Virginia Beach, another city which was only 25 minutes away give or take from Hampton, VA.

Our daughter was 6 months when I moved into my first place and I was extremely excited because though I felt like I had the weight of the world on my shoulders, I was approved for my first place. I was excited and nervous at the same time. I had family in Virginia Beach and in fact one of my sisters lived out the same neighborhood I was getting ready to move into. This wasn't the fanciest apartment but it was mine and something I could afford and would be able to maintain without having to depend on anyone and have them throw it in my face.

I can remember having a conversation with my homegirl and telling her I couldn't wait until my place came through because I was on the waitlist for several months, maybe longer. I was at work one day; I remember it like it was yesterday. I was working at TRG Customer Solutions "club TRG" everyone and their momma worked there literally lol. Anyhow, I asked my homegirl to act like she was me and call to see if I had moved up on the waitlist. I was hopeful but I definitely didn't expect her to call me back with great news. She told me that they said they were just about to call me because I was the next person on the waitlist for the next available two-bedroom apartment and to let me know how much my security deposit was going to be. As you can imagine with the amount of stress and chaos that I had going on in my life this was probably the best news that I had received in such a long time. I made sure to turn in everything that the rental office needed from me and was sure to put money away to make sure I was deposit ready when I got the call about moving. It was August 2010 and my baby girl was six months when I officially moved into my first place. While I was happy and mostly everyone else congratulated me and was happy for me there was certainly one person who wasn't. He felt as if this was a way for me to intentionally keep our daughter from him although the drive with no traffic was all of 20 to 25 minutes give or take.

This was when I was first introduced to "show causes" and this was the very first of many show causes to come. A show cause is supposed to be used or filed when one party violates the custody/visitation agreement. I didn't receive my actual address until maybe a few days before I was due to move in and I made him well aware of this but in spite of knowing all of this he still insisted on filing a show cause with the courts as if I was violating our agreement. Something I never understood and still to this day don't understand is if you don't have the physical address to where you will be located at least 30 days prior to the actual move how in the world can you provide something that you don't have???? I digress!!! If you ask me, it's another big loop hole in our judicial system where someone can run back and forth to court for no apparent reason and file a show cause for no reason and the courts don't require proof before allowing the show cause to be filed.

This became a pattern and what started seemed like every five minutes after a short while. Not only did it mean missing time from work but usually court was an all morning and sometimes afternoon thing so it was certainly not one of my favorite places or things to have to do. Many times, I didn't know what lies would be told in court against me but even though my relationship with God wasn't strong as it is today and it took me A long time to come to this reality and really have an understanding, I was confident in the fact that God was with me and that I had nothing to hide nor worry about because in reality this battle was truly not mines it was the Lord's. I had to remind myself that he was simply using me and that if he brought me to it surely, he was going to see me through it. Eventually the first show cause was thrown out because I didn't refuse to give him the address. I just didn't have the actual apartment number to give to the courts to update the address. As soon as I was given my apartment number I sent him as well the JDR court our new address.. With this court thing somewhat behind me I knew I had to start living a life that would provide better for me and our daughter. I had already enrolled myself in school again and was due to start Saint Leo University that fall which was (August 2010). I wasn't sure how I was going to manage going to school full time, work full time and of course being a mommy all at once but I knew I had to do something and that I wanted more for us. I found myself doing exceptionally well at Saint Leo as I studied for my Bachelor's degree in Healthcare Management. I went to class a few nights a week and worked during the day. There were many days I cried but I just knew I had to keep going despite how hard and tough it got. I soon found out that Saint Leo had a two-track degree program in which I met the requirements for and was on track to walk for my Associates degree in Business Administration while continuing on to finish my Bachelor's degree. In May of 2012 I walked across the stage for my Associates Degree in Business Administration and in May 2014 I walked for my Bachelor's of Science of Health Care Management but I officially completed that degree in August 2014.

In the midst of graduating with both degrees I managed to get pregnant again and I just didn't have the words. Yes, it was by the same man. Everything you may be thinking I heard it all and that's fine it was what it was. I felt ashamed and quite honestly, I didn't want to bring another child into the world especially with him considering everything we had already been through..

This pregnancy was very hard emotionally for me because I dealt with a lot of regret and I just knew I wasn't ready for another child especially knowing some of the trials that their father and I had previously gone through. I found out I was pregnant again by way of a famous Dollar Tree pregnancy test. I remember started to feel nauseous and I was beginning to be increasingly tired more than I normally was and my cycle didn't come on which was a big indicator something was off because I always had regular cycles. Not only did my cycle not come on but every morning I was throwing up when I would go brush my teeth. I prayed that I wasn't pregnant but it was already too late. I was definitely pregnant. I can remember crying and having a host of other emotions. I felt so detached from life and my reality. I already felt bad enough but I knew once word got out that I would be condemned and judged.

I think the first person I told was my best friend at the time. She helped to lift my spirits and told me she was there for me and in that moment that was exactly what I needed to hear. She allowed me to cry and just was present in the moment. When I told others I got what I expected to receive and though it didn't feel good I know I created that environment by allowing others into my business when I was going through everything with their father the first time around. I got the classic "I know you aren't pregnant by him again" I can remember holding my head down in shame and just remembering feeling a sense of me slipping away mentally. I already had to live with the reality of it myself and the weight of my decision and then having to hear the opinions of everyone else especially my loved ones was a hard pill to swallow to say the least. It just was one that I wasn't quite ready to swallow. I eventually made my way to tell their father and he and I both knew this wasn't an ideal situation. He was supportive but there were also times that he denied our son. I just allowed that to go in one ear and out the other. I had ABSOLUTELY NO WORRIES I didn't even get down like that so I was like yeah play in somebody else face like that, not mine. I believe he was only saying it to get to me but I had bigger fish to fry at this point and I needed to stay focused on developing a healthy child, taking care of our daughter and school. The most shame came from some of the conversations I had and here I was right back pregnant again by him. I had to take accountability, it was my fault.

One thing about me I'm going to keep it real cause I was looking really crazy and when I was going through certain things, I just knew I would never be with him like that again but clearly that wasn't the case. You know how you prematurely speak on something or someone for that matter; because you never think you all will get back together especially in that way (intimately). It was at that moment I learned A LOT, at least I thought. I don't say this lightly but, at this moment, I knew I was carrying our unborn child and I was struggling internally to say the least. I felt numb and so detached and I just began to slip into a state of depression. I can remember telling their father "I can't do this and I honestly felt like I didn't want to live anymore." I felt like though he listened and tried to encourage and comfort/console me in the best way that he knew how, there was really nothing he or anymore else could do because there was still this feeling of loneliness, feeling lost and feeling like I was here but not here. I cried many days and nights but somehow and now I know it was by the grace of God that I was able to make it through. I set up an appointment to have a procedure done. Let me back track... This appointment was before anyone really knew I was pregnant and the procedure was scheduled on the last possible day that I could legally have an abortion done in Virginia.

The evening before my appointment, I received a phone call stating that something came up and the person who was supposed to take me could no longer take me. I was not expecting that but life happens and I didn't have time to dwell on it. I had to figure out what I was going to do because there was no way I was turning back at this point or so I thought. I reached out to a sister of mine not knowing what to expect or knowing what she would say. I really didn't have time to really even consider it or care. Though it was very uncomfortable for her, I could tell in her voice as she agreed. Before agreeing though she gave me the third degree and asked me questions about who was supposed to take me initially and why they could no longer take me. With reluctance she agreed to meet me at my house in the morning before the appointment. I was expecting to drive as this sister never liked to drive anywhere but something was different about today and I knew it but I just couldn't put my hand on it at first.

As we proceeded to leave my apartment and head down to my car I proceeded to the driver seat and she stopped me in my tracks and said: "I'll drive today." Surprised, I said "you'll do what now?" She proceeded by saying girl get in the car and come on. So that's exactly what I did. I got in the car and reclined my seat back attempting to try and relax my mind but that seemed nearly impossible. After about 10 mins into the drive I noticed my sister was going the wrong way. I began to question her and she assured me that she knew where she was going and to just sit back. A few minutes later I noticed she was pulling into the neighborhood of one of her friends. At this point I'm not only confused but also irritated because she knew this was the last day that I could get the procedure done and she was about to make me late which automatically would have canceled the appointment. She pulled into a parking space, parked the car and looked at me and said come up stairs with me. I know I must have rolled my eyes super hard in frustration but really what choice did I have at this point. We proceeded to walk up the stairs and her friend met us at the door. I knew this friend and from what I knew of her she always seemed to be a sweetheart in my book but this wasn't what this was about at this point because as far as I was concerned, I didn't know what was going on but whatever it was I wasn't feeling it. She always called me by my last name, she said hey Pooser, come on in and sit down.

Then they hit me with the "we need to talk to you." My sister began to explain that she knows she agreed to take me but after praying about it she couldn't do it. She said "while I can't control you, I couldn't possibly take you and have that blood on my hands." I really didn't fully understand what she meant by that I knew of God but didn't really have an intimate relationship with God at that time. I had to come to terms with this because this meant that though I hadn't mentally prepared for what if I didn't get an abortion this was now my reality. They talked to me and consoled me as the tears just began streaming down my face as the weight of what I was about to do set in. They both encouraged me saying that I was a great mother and I was doing a great job with my daughter and I would also be a great mother to this child as well. I listened to everything they had to say and the tears would not stop streaming down my face. I eventually stopped crying and got myself together and shortly thereafter my sister and I left her friend's house. I think I went in the house, got something to eat and drank some water and just relaxed the remainder of the day before my daughter was due to come back home. I believe once I accepted it in my mind I was able to embrace the fruit of my womb. Though I didn't know when and how I just knew that somehow again hopefully sooner than later I would be okay.

When my daughter came home I fed her, gave her a bath and we cuddled up on the couch watching cartoons until we both fell asleep. Once she was sound asleep, I put her in the bed and took my shower and got in the bed next to her. That night was probably the best night of sleep that I had received in a long time. It was as if a huge weight had been lifted off of my shoulders and I felt a sense of peace. I faced some ridicule but that was okay. I believe I addressed it one good time and left it alone. Everyone was entitled to their opinions and it just let me know I had to make sure that I made a way to provide a good and stable life for them the best way I could. The months quickly flew by and we found out we were having a baby boy. He was excited that he was going to have a little man. He was proud carrying the ultrasound picture around "talking about you see my little man." Though things weren't perfect things started to look up for a little while.

    At about six or seven months we got into an argument about a secret that was withheld from me. I was furious because with all the mess I went through... we would have never even been together if I had known and been given a choice in the matter. This secret was apparently only a secret to me. I came across a message in which I found out he was legally still married. I was never the snooping type because if I have to do all of that then clearly we don't need to be together but this was one of those things that fell in my lap. His Facebook was left open on the computer to the message of the woman who was apparently still legally wife. When I asked him about the messages and the marriage his response was it was an arranged marriage when he was in the military that did not mean anything to him. He also tried to convince me I knew. I can't even explain the thoughts that were going through my head. As sure as my name is Shalil I would have never knowingly messed with a married man. I don't care what type of marriage it was and even if he was separated. All I could think about is the level of betrayal and why didn't anyone in his family think it was important to tell me or even find out if I knew. I can remember crying, feeling hurt and betrayed and most of all just stupid. All I could think was what did I get myself into and whatever it was it was too late here I was pregnant with this man's second child and just just finding out about a marriage that he was still legally tied to.

    When I found out his whole family knew and just assumed I knew I was taken aback because why did they feel and assume I knew? What led them to even begin to think this way, had he convinced them this was true..? I reached out to her to see if I could get some truth about the matter and I was very respectful and she was at first too. Later word got back to his family that I reached out to her and they accused me of creating drama when in reality all I wanted was the truth, I felt like in the very least I deserved that. I really couldn't believe this was happening to me like what in the world and how? I can remember calling my best friend at the time and just pouring out to her. She allowed me to just vent and provided a listening ear and kept apologizing as if it was somehow her fault and telling me I would get through this. I did my best to get through the rest of this pregnancy and that semester of school that I was currently enrolled in.

In February 2012 which was the month before I was due, I was involved in a car accident in which by the grace of God both parties had only minor injuries because judging from the looks of both cars there was no way we should have been able to walk out of the cars. I just had some minor scarring to my right knee and my stomach banged against the steering wheel so my only concern was really for my son. I was so thankful that my daughter was not with me because the car was hit really hard on the side where I would most of the time place her car seat and the airbags deployed all over the car. Something told me to leave her home and I was so grateful that I did leave her at my house with my sister that morning because she came over to visit.

I got to the hospital and the doctor checked on both my son and I. I was nervous because he was a very active baby and it felt like after the accident, he stopped moving so fear began to grip me. I was relieved when they performed the ultrasound and confirmed that he was still alive and healthy. The doctor said you have a healthy baby boy and he is a fighter. I was grateful that we were not only alive but we were both in good health. The others involved in the accident were also fine. The lady's son did have a nose bleed though. Once I was released from the hospital, I went home and showered and just tried to relax as best as I could but I was still a little bit shaken up and I was trying to wrap my head around everything as it happened so fast. The next day the reality hit me that I was now eight months pregnant and though I was provided a rental car for a week or so I no longer had a car. I already knew it was going to be a struggle to get another because the position I was working in ended a couple of months prior and going to the dealership without pay stubs and trying to get another car was nearly impossible. I definitely didn't have enough saved up to just go get another car and what I did have saved up was enough to cover my bills for the next couple of months and to ensure me and my babies would be able to get what we needed.

Thankfully I had family and friends that were willing to help me out as much as possible with doctors' appointments, getting back and forth to school and other places that were absolutely necessary. It was very easy to get discouraged and I just began thinking about pulling out of school for the rest of the semester but I was so glad that my dad encouraged me to keep going and I was graced with the endurance to continue and finish that semester strong. I hated to ask for anything so having to rely on anyone for a ride was very hard but I swallowed my pride and asked for help because I really needed it. My due date was March 22, 2012 but I started having contractions on March the 10th. I've always had a high pain tolerance so as best as I could I tried to brush them off as I really thought they were just braxton hicks contractions. I can remember going to use the bathroom and what I later found out was my mucus plug fell out. I called the doctor on call because I wasn't sure what that was and I didn't experience that happening with my pregnancy with my daughter. The doctor assured me it was normal and there was nothing to worry about but to head to the hospital if I started experiencing too much pain and thought I was going into labor. This was probably about 6:30 P.M that Saturday evening. I can remember just trying my best to focus on finishing my term paper before calling it a night.

As I was sitting on the couch working on my paper I began to experience excruciating contractions so I went ahead and called their father and my parents to see who could get me to the hospital first. They all were in Hampton and I lived in Virginia Beach and needed to deliver at Sentara Princess Anne. The drive was not long but when you are having back-to-back contractions it seems like forever. I can remember being in the back seat leaned up against the door and my sister was asking me questions knowing I wasn't in the mood to answer any questions lol. The contractions had intensified at this point and every turn my dad made I felt. I remember rocking back and forth trying my best to take my mind off of the pain. I believe I was able to make contact with my parents first and him shortly after I was in the car with my parents.

We arrived at the hospital, got checked in and their father beat me to the hospital and was already waiting in the waiting area for us to arrive. After I got checked in at the main lobby I was sent upstairs to labor and delivery for them to check me and found out I was 4cms dilated and that they were going to keep me. This meant that we would have him sometime tomorrow as it was already 11 P.M. I was ready for the pain to be over but the reality was the next day I was no longer going to be only a mother of one but now a mother of two. I was able to go all the way natural with my daughter without any medication but baby it's something about that second child that hit me differently and seemed to be more painful than my first experience with being in labor. The pain was really intense and I couldn't handle it anymore so they had the anesthesiologist come in and give me an epidural. I heard so many stories about how you have to be extremely still so you won't become paralyzed so I made sure to be as still as I possibly could be. As expected, it took a few minutes for the epidural to kick in and then I was finally able to relax while in labor until it was time for me to push. When it was time for me to push, he came out on the second push. The only thing I remember is being filled with happiness and a sigh of relief that he was brought into the world safe and neither one of us had any major complications.

It happened so fast I remember telling the doctor "don't drop my baby," as I laid back because I was clearly still highly medicated from the epidural. I looked over and could see the proud look on their dad's face as he said "I have my lil man." I really wanted to name him Adrian and I was stuck on it but when they asked me what his name was going to be I realized despite how much we had been through at the end of the day it was still his child just as much as it was mine and I didn't want to take away that moment as he wanted our son to be named after him. Our baby boy made his entrance into this world at 5:30 am on Sunday March 11, 21012. I can remember having of course my mom, dad, their father, and two of my sisters there and later that day I received a few more visitors. Something about giving birth this time around felt very different and I began to feel really lonely and feel the weight of not having the type of support I wanted and needed from those who meant a lot to me. Their dad had to leave later in the day to get ready for work and came back later with his mom and our daughter so she could meet her baby brother. As you could imagine she was excited to meet him and take on her role as his big sister. She was given the nickname "Boss Lady" for a reason. After they left, just me and our baby boy were left alone and had some bonding time. I just took this quiet time to soak in the reality of everything after completing some homework. My professor was really impressed that I even considered doing my homework considering the fact that I had just given birth and gave me extra credit on top of my regular grade. I was very grateful for that and it gave me even more motivation to keep going as I was so close to the finish line of walking for my Associates degree and I was determined to make it happen!

The next day I received a call and a visit from one of my older sisters and my best friend at the time. They brought some things for the baby. My sister came by briefly but she couldn't stay long. My friend stayed for about an hour and we caught up and talked about plans for the future. I waited all day for their dad to come to the hospital and time must have gotten away from him because day grew into night. I tried to remain calm but my emotions got the best of me and I definitely let him have it when he got there. When he got there, he said he was tired because he was playing basketball and got injured. All I could do is stare at him like you have got to be kidding me. I just let him know how I was truly feeling and then listened to what he had to say and just decided to leave it alone because it was really a waste of time at this point.

He held our baby for a few minutes before giving him back to me so he could latch on. I put our baby to sleep and placed him back in the crib at the hospital and paged the nurse to keep an eye on him while I took a nap until it was time for his next feeding. His dad fell asleep in the chair at the hospital. He ended up leaving that night and at that point I didn't care I just knew I was ready to go home and get focused back on my goals, welcoming our baby boy home and start adjusting to life now as a mother of two children. The next day came and when afternoon came, we were released to go home.

I can remember going home and I thought I was going home to relax and try to recover. My plans did not go as such because I had to make dinner, straighten up and make sure the kids were good to go. He was out for hours despite knowing that I was trying to recover from being fresh out of the hospital with a newborn and a one-year-old who was about to turn two in less than two weeks. Whatever he had going on was evidently more important than making sure my load was lightened. I can remember when he walked in the house that evening, I was exhausted. I didn't even have the strength nor energy to argue, I just asked a few questions and left it alone because at this point there was no point. I began cleaning up the kitchen and he said relax I got it but I was like nope I'm good at this point.

I proceeded to finish cleaning my kitchen, took a shower and got some rest while he sat with our son until it was time for his next feeding. Despite everything going on I was excited that I was able to breastfeed this time around because after the hospital gave our daughter a bottle, I could no longer get her to latch on after that. I knew from very early on as early as 3 days old that our son was going to be a very demanding child. He would do this thing with his head when I didn't feed him fast enough and had a very strong grip very early on. Trying to adjust to breastfeeding was not for the weak. He was that newborn that most definitely ate on schedule every few hours. He was the complete opposite of his sister as a newborn because I had to wake her up most of the time for her feedings when she slept too long.

Welcoming another baby in what felt like storms were raging all around me, I was reminded of what I now know as My Heavenly Father and I was filled with joy and every tear I cried was suddenly worth it. Holding my baby, I just knew I was holding a precious jewel, a precious king that would later be a force to be reckoned with. The bonding experience that a mother and child experience due to breastfeeding is a feeling that I would most certainly recommend to every mother if they are able to breastfeed. Outside of the bonding experience if offered to the mother and the child it has other benefits such as decreasing the chances that your child will get sick, helps to fight infections immediately after birth, helps the mother drop belly weight faster and a host of other benefits. The breast is also used as a natural healing agent for certain things. I experienced a different type of love having a baby boy and I absolutely adore my daughter as well. She was a blessing and still is a blessing from God but having a son was just different. Boys truly love and don't play about their mommas. I will say that oftentimes and it was absolutely my experience, breastfed babies tend to be more spoiled and clingier. When I held him in my arms for the first time it was love at first sight. He was so precious and cute and I thanked God. He was perfect.

I asked their father to leave my place the same week that I gave birth because I was always told you can do bad by yourself. We would go on to go through too many court cases to count on both hands. He would try to control me through our children when he couldn't have his way. I would often call his fits temper tantrums because it literally reminded me of how a child would act when they couldn't have their way. I mean this man filed show cause after show cause and I was so frustrated with the court systems. I never understood the fact that anyone could be allowed to just file showcases without some sort of evidence because Hampton JDR would literally have you in court alllllllllll day long. It didn't matter to him that I was missing work and ultimately money to help provide for our children. It became very apparent that he didn't want to see me get ahead, which didn't make any sense because I had our kids primarily. I digress. I won't go through every court case but there was this one in particular that I'll never forget as long as I live. God showed me that he was in fact my lawyer in the courtroom. It wasn't just a cliche' saying but it became my reality when my back was against the wall and all odds were stacked against me. It was nobody but God, I'm talking about MY God. Not the little one but I'm talking about Big GOD!!!!

I had just transitioned from one job to another and this was when I was hired as A TC or supervisor with Optima Health. My old supervisor just so happened to be my manager here. I was thankful for this and it became very important and I'll tell you why. So as previously mentioned, I stayed in court with this man and my sister showed up every time I'll forever love her for that. My manager was already familiar with what was going on with my relationship with their dad because I had to either keep leaving work or missing work for court. Court was fastly approaching once again and this time I said I want a lawyer. My goal was to put a stop to all this back and forth when he couldn't have his way. It was draining!!!

My manager introduced me to someone who had a really good custody/visitation lawyer due to a recent divorce I believe. She was really nice. I didn't appreciate him telling my business as I didn't know her but that was neither here nor there. I just wanted this behind me cause I was honestly tired of him playing with me and me just having to keep going through this battle in court for nothing at all. She introduced me to a lawyer after I had to fire the lawyer I previously had that was never supposed to take on my case. I'll explain...

Their dad would literally tell the courts lie after lie. I mean I would be in there appalled wondering what would come out of his mouth next. One time he even lied and had CPS called on me all because I finally put him on child support and the arrears quickly added up. I should have been a bitter woman as much as I went through but I just wasn't built like that. It was my goal to level up and provide a better life for me and my babies. That was it and that was all. He told CPS that I was getting speeding tickets and my kids weren't in car seats and I would have my 10 yr old niece watch our children. You know how they say when you hear a lie about yourself you have to laugh because baby I was amazed. I used to tell myself this man is really in the wrong business. Surely he was supposed to be a fiction story teller or even an actor winning an oscar or something cause what sir. I'm like you said I did what now? Tell me more! He told me one time on facebook if I gave our daughter the name she has he would hate me forever and I guess he sat out to prove just that!

Anyhow, we are fastly approaching court. I just began this new position and I needed a lawyer. I reached out to my homegirl (or so I thought) who was in law school or had just recently graduated. She was my cousin's best friend but we had known each other since middle school. She referred me to a lawyer and to unbeknownst to me this lawyer was never supposed to take on my case. She took on my case knowing she knew their father all along. In fact she was in the same band as him in high school so how did she not know?? Things that make you go hmmmm. My cousin's best friend gave me the attorney's information and naturally I called her and she asked me for all these details about the children and what I was looking for as a result of this case. We discussed in great detail the outcome I was looking for and my ultimate goal which was to stop the back and forth in court and a custody order that would accommodate the both of us. I went to her office and signed my retainer and one of the things she asked me for when she asked me his name was do you have a picture of him.

At this point I didn't think it was strange at all I thought maybe it was just protocol of some sort.

Time would go on. I did my part by giving her everything she asked for and checked in when asked etc., One day my friend was like how is everything going with the lawyer so far. I said you know I haven't really been hearing much from her, maybe I should check in to ensure everything is still good to go. By this time we were maybe a month or so out from court. I sent her an email just inquiring about the progress of the case and there was a shift in her demeanor as if I was somehow now her enemy. She began to say I hadn't been complying but I had other emails telling me otherwise so it didn't make sense at all. Maybe another week or two went by and I got a call one day while I was in training from her so I stepped out to take the call. The call went left very quickly. She accused me of not being upfront and honest with her about things. I was completely lost as to what she was even talking about. She went on to tell me that it is the recommendation of the GAL to not have our children removed from Hampton city schools as the children were doing exceptionally well and our daughter was in a gifted program. She said that it was the GAL position to side with their father. She said I initially told the GAL that I was moving to Virginia beach but I ended up moving to Norfolk. I was looking in both cities but ultimately found a place in Norfolk first. She went on to ask if I already knew he had the kids registered in Hampton. I advised her it shouldn't have been done because he was made aware well ahead of time that I was relocating for a better job opportunity. She went on to say it's not looking good for me and unless I could give her some HARD evidence against him it was not going to go in my favor. All while in the midst of all of this she advised me that he contacted her asking for her to represent him on this same case and she had her staff advise him that she already represented me on this case so it was not possible. She went on to tell me that he was very rude to her staff so that made her want to represent me even more… the lies she told whew! She went on to say that "he demanded that she drop me as a client. She was his lawyer and she had previously represented him in other cases." But remember she didn't know him though??? Things that make you go hmmm. But wait, during one of my fasts the Holy Spirit revealed to me that who I often referred to and actually loved like a sister (my cousin's best friend) did in fact know more than she led me to believe and set the plan in motion. I was like God... huh I got a sunken feeling in my stomach and couldn't believe what I was hearing. I literally had no words. The Holy Spirit hadn't revealed this right away. I believe had I been in the position to hear clearly I would have known a lot sooner. BUT GOD!!!!

Y'all couldn't possibly understand the weight and heaviness I was feeling because how is it that my lawyer who is supposed to be working for me now telling me it's not looking good based off of the GAL wanting the children to stay in hampton. My heart sank. I cried, prayed and some more. I went to a "prayer room" with my friend at the time. I went into what they called the soaking room after signing up and then had to write my prayer requests down and wait to be called. They called me in and they asked for my hands and surrounded me to pray. I can't remember all they said but I remember them telling me that the Victory was already won and that my enemies had me surrounded on every side. They also said God said "GET OUT OF YOUR FLESH, GET OUT OF YOUR FLESH, THIS IS SPIRITUAL." I mean the weight of power she said it in I trembled and buckled under the sound of her voice. Whew. She said and as far as that lawyer "it's much more to it than that." I'm sure you can put two and two together to make four!!!!!

That was all I needed to know as far as the lawyer. I knew she wasn't forthcoming at all and she wasn't integral at all. I ended up doing her a favor. I called her and started asking her about my case, her relationship with him and a host of other questions. She immediately became defensive and said well Ms. Pooser if you don't trust me then maybe we shouldn't continue this relationship as client and attorney. I said you are exactly right. I would like for you to remove yourself from my case and I would like to request my retainer back since you never worked on my case anyway. She ended up refunding my money but of course she did it by way of her office staff cause I really wanted to fight at this point because now you are playing with my kids and me at this point but I picked up my money and left. I also found that she had never even registered with the courts as my lawyer. I mean this lady was really trying to railroad me but GOD! I cried, I was frustrated and devastated. I called my cousin's best friend and she kept apologizing and saying I'm so sorry and crying. At this time I didn't know she really knew the plot that was set up against me and that she was in on it.

I got some information from another lawyer on the best way to prepare but it was literally two days away from court and she didn't have time to prepare for my case. I was very appreciative of what she did share with me because it blessed me tremendously and helped me to represent myself of course with the Help of the Holy Spirit. God was my lawyer in the courtroom and no one can tell me anything differently. I took all of her advice she gave freely since it was too late to take on my case.

I set out to win this case and I was determined to do just that! She suggested I go all the way from the beginning and just outline as specific as possible. I literally stayed at work until about 10pm of course once I finished my work just working on preparing for my case. I got everything typed up and laid out. I went into that courtroom with my briefcase and baby you couldn't tell me I wasn't a lawyer. The evening before I went to go get my babies from his house. When I pulled up my daughter came out but something was very different about our son. I asked him to come on and get in the car and he was acting differently, something I had never seen before. He ran around the car, he was just not himself. He was kicking and screaming saying he didn't want to come. So their grandma (his mom) came outside and said oh he can stay or something like that. I was too tired so I just let him stay and said I'll get to the bottom of it after court. Court was the next morning. Their father also said oh so I see you tried to hire my lawyer? I'm looking puzzled and oh so confused cause what do you mean I tried to hire your lawyer? He went on to mention her name. I was like excuse me? He mentioned yeah my homegirl told me you tried to hire her as your lawyer and she is not going to represent you. Oh okay so now it was all beginning to make perfect sense BUT GOD! They even tried to lie and tell me court was continued to a new date but the reality of it was it wasn't. They hoped I wouldn't show up but by this time I didn't believe I believed anything he said without hard proof.

I had prepared for court. Now, it was just time to pray and have faith to believe that God was going to be my lawyer in the courtroom and doing exceedingly, abundantly above what I could ask or think. The court proceedings started when the GAL presented her case and you would have thought she was his personal lawyer how hard she was going for him. I sat there and listened to all the evidence being presented and when it was my turn I pulled out my briefcase and all my evidence to include emails of text messages and pics I had from this man and how he talked to me. I also just poured my heart out to the judge. I must have been talking too fast because he said "Ms. Pooser, take a deep breath, I hear you calm down, it's going to be okay." I gathered myself and continued. My sister took the stand, then his mom came into the courtroom and took the stand. I believe they asked her why she feels like their dad should get primary custody and she went on to say something no one could have prepared me for. She said "I don't know what is going on in her house but I never saw my grandson act the way that he did when she came to pick him up. " This suggested to the court that I was doing something to him. I couldn't believe my ears because if this was really the case why hadn't they taken measures to take the kids forreal and why would my daughter who is older not be affected by "what I had going on in my home". Again, I digress.

The judge said after hearing all of the evidence on both sides I am going to keep primary custody with the mother and I cried tears of Joy! All I could say was thank you, your Honor! I knew he saw through all of the lies and manipulation. All odds were stacked up against me and even the GAL recommendation didn't stand a chance when it came to fighting up against one of God's CHOSEN. I got all kinds of nasty stares from him, his mom and the GAL and baby I did not care one bit! I told my cousin's best friend about the case and she said "girl do you know you just hurt that GAL's record?" (Again at this time I didn't know she was in on it…) I said I didn't but next time she better play with someone else and not me cause when it comes to my babies I'm never going to play! ALL GLORY BE TO GOD! I was simply a vessel he chose to use at that moment. That took my faith to another level and I was so grateful for that! I had experienced God in a way that I had never experienced the POWER of God before! Like I knew God was good but to have all odds stacked against me and still come out VICTORIOUS was like wow this is really real! I suggest before going up against one of God's CHOSEN with a pure heart before God to find you something safe to do. This was around September of 2017.

Chapter 2

My Battle with Depression/ Winning the battle Within me

My battle with depression really began as a little girl but I really didn't understand until later down the line as the older generation might say by and by. I slept a lot and I really enjoyed sleeping and if I'm being completely honest I still enjoy sleeping cause baby one thing about me I'm going to take a nap lol. I just now have the wisdom to understand when my sleeping or me feeling the need to sleep is an attack from the enemy and when it's natural because sleep is essential or God is giving me a season of rest from labor.

The Holy Spirit revealed to me a few years ago during a time of prayer and fasting that sleeping was the enemy's way of holding me back from what God had for me. I mean the sleep felt so good I could sleep for hours, wake up for a little while and find myself sleepy all over again. I used to be like there's no way cause I just woke up. This cycle continued in my life for many many years until the Holy Spirit gave me understanding of exactly what was going on. I was also depressed because of my lazy eyes and skin problems and of course the generation we live in everything is about vain things that God is not even concerned with. This doesn't mean that God caused my skin to be less than perfect but he allowed it and if he allowed it. Though I'm working on my skin care goals, my skin care I thank God that he fixed my heart in the situation. I love me because God first loved me in spite of myself. He saved a wretch like me.

Oftentimes I would lay and cry and in my own mind I still couldn't understand why?

I thought to myself and began to pray: Holy Spirit you are welcome here in this place and space speak to me, I'm ready to be set free! God it's me again I need you so desperately to rescue me from my own thoughts and memories of what I thought were defeat. Silence my mind so I can hear you speak. I would begin to put God in remembrance of his word. God, you said that "ALL things work for the good of those that love you and are called according to your purpose." God you can do EVERYTHING but fail. Your word reminds me that in you I'm more than a conqueror and as Jesus has overcome the whole world that same power lies within me through Jesus Christ. It's in you that I have victory over the enemy. It is in you that I live, move and have my being (Acts 17:28). So, God change my mind, heart and perspective. I pray for humility so I can humbly walk with you to do whatever it is that you ask and task me to do.

I had experienced a season of tremendous loss. Not to death in the natural but by way of people being removed from my life mostly because our season had just run its course. I began to go through a season of learning and unlearning some things and behaviors. I just learned about the wisdom in being quiet so I could hear clearly and so I could heal without bleeding on people that didn't hurt me.

So often we fight the process of being alone or being in solitude, consecrated before God but sometimes it is so necessary! Both praying and fasting is a must for growth spiritually. Matthew 17:21 "But this kind does not go out except by prayer and fasting." We have to die to ourselves daily, crucify our flesh, Jesus said take up your cross and follow me. He did not say follow your pastors, bishops, best friends but take up your cross and follow me. He said seek ye first the kingdom of Heaven and all of its righteousness and then all of these things will be added unto you. It was in that time of solitude and consecration that God really began showing me what was housed in my heart and what spirits were dwelling on the inside of me. I began to pray God make like a child in you again. God I'm not sure I fully understand how to totally submit, relinquish control and humble myself before you. God, I need you to show me, Holy Spirit, teach me how to do the will of My Father.

At this time, I went into praise giving thanksgiving to God just for who he is. I began: God thank you for who you are… God you are the lifter of my head. You are Holy, you are righteous, you are omniscient, you are omnipotent, you are the light in the darkness, you are a miracle worker, you are a way maker, you are my fortress, you are the Alpha and Omega, you are my beginning and me end, you are the author and finisher of my faith. God you are Worthy to be Praised. I continued to Praise him but you get the gist of it. I asked God to silence my own thoughts that did not align with his word so I could hear his voice louder than any other voice. I began to put God in remembrance of his word again and say: "You said all things work together for the good of those who love you and are called according to YOUR PURPOSE!" God you can do EVERYTHING but fail! Your word reminds me that in you I'm more than a conqueror and as you have overcome the world that some power lies within me through Christ Jesus, I have the Victory. I have been set free.

God, I need you to change my mind and appetite. I pray for humility so I can humbly walk with you to do whatever it is that you ask me to do. As I began to really get into the word of God more and more and not just read my daily devotions it literally made a difference. The hunger and thirst for more of God (His Holy Word) grew even more. If I had a question about a specific subject matter or was facing a specific issue that I wanted to know what the Word of God said concerning that situation, I literally googled scriptures to help seeks what his word says regarding the situation and asked The person of The Holy Spirit to give me revelation of what was going on in the spiritual realm and what this meant pretty much to give me clarity on what I was reading so I would not lean to my own understanding.

I admit I have been guilty of this several times. It is so easy if we're not mindful and can error on the side of becoming prideful if we aren't careful. When I really began to make a habit of doing this and remaining consistent in my pursuit of God the Word of God became more evident in my life like never before. It may sound cliché or like duh Shalil but I would say all the time I need to go home and get in the word and do everything else, but get in my word. The times I did start I would almost always become completely distracted from the reading of the word. I would get on a good track but then I would start struggling to follow a routine and I was never really consistent and persistent enough to see the kind of breakthrough that I was really needing and believing in God for.

During covid 2020 I literally had no more excuse. I began to write while sitting up in my bed and some scriptures began to scream at me. I made it my business to learn them and then apply them for surely the Holy Spirit was speaking to me and knew exactly what I needed as those very scriptures seemed to jump out at me.

The first one was Matt 12:36-37 and the second was Matt 12:34-35 It was after reading these scriptures that it hit me like a ton of bricks. It was then that I realized maybe I hadn't really healed. I was always speaking about what happened to me, how it wasn't fair and trying to show my innocence in situations but little did I know it was making me look worse and furthermore I was sinning by gossiping and sowing seeds of discord. I realized that I was so focused on the outer core that I was missing what God was trying to do on the inner core (on the inside) for we know that God deals with the heart of man. I was so focused on what I wanted God to heal or change about me physically that I neglected to see how broken I was internally. So often we can easily see what's wrong with others and we are quick to point out other people's mess but I'm reminded of the word that says in Matthew 7:5 you hypocrite, first take the plank out of your own eye, and then you will see clearly to remove the speck from your brother's eye.

Now this does not excuse you from speaking on those things in which God has caused you to speak about and bring warning. Oftentimes when people come for us, we want to clap back and the temptation is always real especially when you feel justified in doing so but we must realize that just like we have struggles and burdens that we face others do as well. We should however instead ask God to help us to sharpen our gift of discerning of spirits or help us to bring everything before him in prayer so that we may righteously judge a situation and not lean to our own understanding. We give the enemy too much room and footing on us when we make what was a simple misunderstanding and become offended. This opens the door for the spirit of offense to be housed in our hearts which opens other doors spiritually sometimes bitterness and anger.

If you are someone who has struggled with this, pray this prayer with me: Father, I come to you as humble as I know how, I stretch my hands to thee the only help I know. God thank you for loving me and keeping me. God you are gracious, you are loving and kind. God, you sit high and you look low. God you are the potter and I am the clay. Father forgive me for my sinful ways, God I repent for taking matters into my own hands, God forgive me for gossiping, spreading seeds of discord, God forgive me for unrighteously judging a situation (not judging it according to righteous judgment) judging situations with my natural eyes instead of my spiritual eyes. Father forgive me for judging a situation with my carnal mind (flesh) and not allowing the Holy Spirit to guide me in this matter. Father help me to be a better listener and not so quick to speak. God I know it's not enough to just say sorry but God I ask that you give me a repentant heart. God search my heart and anything that's not like you I pray and ask that you take it away.

To repent not only means to ask for forgiveness but to turn from that sin/your sinful ways.

God it is my prayer that you meet each person that will read this book right where they are. God some people are barely holding on, some people are sick in their bodies, God someone is afraid to come back to their first love because of what someone told them, because of condemnation from others or maybe they just feel as if they have strayed too far away. Father touch them from the bottom of their heads to the souls of their feet and do spiritual surgery on their heart. God allow your Holy spirit to give them the peace that only comes from you and that they stand in the need of. Lead and guide them into the truths of your holy and righteous word. Father allow them to put you back in first place. Father, my prayer is that it be all of you and none of me. May I decrease that you may increase. Fill them with your Holy Spirit as they accept Jesus Christ as their personal savior. May the Holy Spirit rest, rule, and abide in them. It's in Jesus' name that I seal this prayer. Amen.

Chapter 3
(Abortion) Shedding of Innocent Blood (2015)

Well, let me first start off by saying if I had my own way this would have been a chapter and a past memory of my life that I would have taken to the grave with me. I also understand more and more and day by day as I walk with God it's NOT ABOUT ME but about My Heavenly Father's good and perfect and pleasing will for my life. I was in WORSHIP/WARSHIP in my kitchen during a time of fasting and praying and I clearly heard the Holy Spirit say: "Abortion/The Shedding of innocent blood. This was so significant because I was praying that God would not make me open up to the world about this as it was very personal. I began speaking back to the Holy Spirit "Are you sure that you are sure cause nah.. Lol that's how me and God talk sometimes. We have a relationship for real for real not for play-play. In a still small voice I could hear the repeating of the same chapter title as to say don't play with me I said what I said. I'm like wheww okay God if you bring me to it, I know you're going to see me through it. I quickly got out of my feelings as they are fickle and our hearts are deceptive.

I was reminded of Christ's ultimate sacrifice and what if he told his Father I hear what you are saying you need me to do but nah but that's not what I want to do. Song says "Where would I be" I would be like a ship without a sail tossed to and from with no sense of direction. Again, he reminded me that it was not about me but he needed me to be vulnerable and transparent because he needed others to know because they have had an abortion, he has not thrown them away and it is not the unpardonable sin. That is that if they will come running to God with a heart of repentance and turn away from the sin, he is just and faithful to forgive the sin and remember it no more.

He continued on…though this sin is one of the things that I hate and detest, I still have compassion and mercy on my children and those I choose to have compassion and mercy on. He said My grace is sufficient. He continued I want them to know that I still love them and I want to have an intimate and personal relationship with them. I want them to humble themselves before me and seek my face. "Humble yourself before The Lord and seek my face, REPENT and turn from your wicked ways." He says" I don't want them to continue to get abortions. I don't want them to take this lightly. I need my people to STOP joking about this on social media as if it's a laughing matter because it's not funny to SPIT IN MY FACE.

My Story about how I would get my first and last abortion was not something by far that I was proud of. In fact, I have to be completely transparent and honest in saying I was completely against them until I was placed in a position that I felt strongly about needing one. Even after I repented, I still walked around in shame and I set myself down for several months. Many people asked Hey Shalil why haven't you been on Facebook but the truth is I needed God to heal me in private without the noise of others. The bible declares that we are overcome by the blood of the lamb and the word of our testimony. Who the son sets free is truly free indeed. I repented and vowed to God that I would never do it again and I never have.

I can't speak for anyone else but my experience was not a good one at all. I was about 7 weeks pregnant and I wasn't at all prepared for what was to come, even though the procedure was explained to me. As I waited in the waiting room to be called back to the room to have the procedure done I had so many thoughts going through my head. I have to be honest in saying it was a dumb decision and the reason for having it was because I couldn't fathom the thought of having a third child by this man. I beat myself for even placing myself in the predicament of even being in the position to get pregnant again by him. However, it did happen and here I was.

I remember shortly before I found myself pregnant again what I felt like was a breakthrough in his life happening as he was beginning to build a relationship with his father that previously had not been existent in his life to my knowledge. When we talked, he seemed as if he got the apology that he needed and that seemed to be the ice breaker to the little boy that was still hurting down on the inside that any child may have when you have either an absent parent or one who is not consistent. He began to talk about how he wanted his family back and how he wanted to start going to church as a family. My thought process.. clearly leaning on my own understanding, if we both had forgiven the past and were starting a clean slate, we would be good right? So, I thought and that was extremely short lived.

He came over to my house one Saturday we chilled and once the kids were asleep, he made his way into my room. I did try to resist at first because I already knew this wasn't the right thing to do but I did give in to temptation. I asked him about protection and of course he didn't have any so I was like oh nah I'm good. I wasn't on birth control because I wasn't having sex and surely, I wasn't planning on having any more babies. He continued so I began to relax my mind while also rolling my eyes cause what in the world was I thinking; clearly I wasn't thinking. I eventually tried to relax and that turned into panic because he didn't even attempt to "pull out" but got up and made a gesture and whispered yeah I got you. He told me he was going to go to Walgreens to get me the Morning after pill and that didn't happen. I had just finished taking care of my bills and really didn't have the extra funds, it simply wasn't in the budget.

I didn't hear from him until later that evening and he gave me some lame excuse that something happened back in Hampton, VA. I waited and waited for him to send the money through account transfer and kept telling me he would but he never did. Talking about someone being hot as fish grease whew. I was really upset and instantly became filled with regret saying to myself this is what my dumb self gets because I knew better anyway. I couldn't believe I allowed myself to be back right here because again I knew better but obviously wasn't thinking straight. I don't know if I was more upset with him for what I felt like was a set up or for myself for being stuck on stupid.

I was able to get the money like a day later to get the Morning after pill and in the midst of that I found out he was talking to someone shortly after. I just hoped and prayed "Lord please don't let me be pregnant." Well, I must have sent that prayer up just a little too late because a few weeks passed and my cycle never came and my breasts started aching really bad and became really tender to the touch. I was like NOOOOOO this is not happening because I have always had a normal and regular cycle so certainly my cycle not coming raised great concerns for me. I went to the good ole dollar tree one day after my children and I had come from having a day of family time at Mount Trashmore Park. I told them both to go pick out one item and I grabbed two pregnancy tests just to be on the safe side. I went home and got my children settled, fed, and bathed in preparation for bed and then proceeded to take the pregnancy test. What seemed like immediately the test came back to show a positive result. I was filled with grief and sadness because this was a lot to process. I didn't want to be going through this again and certainly not with him. I don't think the timing could have been any worse as it was close to both of our Childrens' birthdays in March. I told one person which shall remain nameless. She let me know she didn't agree with abortion either but in considering EVERYTHING it was probably the best but of course ultimately it was up to me.

To any woman that may read this and you have had an abortion I want you to first forgive yourself of the guilt and shame that you may have walked around in much like I did. I want you to ask for forgiveness and repent which means to not only ask for forgiveness of the sinful act but to turn away from repeating the same act again. Renounce this covenant which means you come out of agreement with it. "I renounce the blood sacrificial covenant that I made with Molech (Demon) and replace it with the Holy Spirit (your covenant to the one and only true and living God). The scriptures that you may reference and ask the Holy Spirit for revelation and take this into prayer are Leviticus 18:21, Deuteronomy 12:31, and Ezekiel 16:20-21.

Chapter 4

What Happens when you didn't ask for the calling on your life to be A Prophetess called to the Nations

When the Holy Spirit Gave me this title, I was like "Wow God, this is so fitting because what in the world?" For much of my life I did not understand many things that I went through and to be completely honest I thought it was unfair. From a young child I have had words spoken over my life; now I know some were from true prophets of God and some were not and were on assignment by the enemy. If I may be completely honest, much of those words spoken didn't make any sense and oftentimes left me confused and carrying a burden that God never intended for me to carry. I unknowingly carried these burdens due to me trying to figure out why I always felt different and asking why I never really "fit in." I also carried a burden because someone said you are going to have a powerful ministry and cause many to come to Christ. In my mind I'm like who is?

I'll never forget this prophet came up to me and my sister when we were out having lunch with my baby girl. She was only 1 at the time. She said, "Can I talk to you for a moment?" I looked around and said, "Who me?" She said yes, you. She went on to say God wants you to go around your house and PRAISE and WORSHIP him giving him all the Glory and that's all she said. I received it because from a young child I always had this love for Gospel music but it all began to make sense because when I'm at home in PRAISE and WORSHIP I experience the presence of GOD so strong that I never want to leave. Like I want to stay in WORSHIP all day. I understand you can still stay in Worship to God without music but it's just something about music we go together real bad lol, if you know you know. I used to get in trouble for playing my music too loud. Like I need it to get down deep on the inside for what I have experienced in this thing called life because life be life-ing!

It wouldn't be until many years later that I discovered that it is the truth of God's word that set me free in letting me know that the burden of the Lord was light. He says: "Come to me, all you who are weary and burdened, and I will give you rest. Take my yoke upon you and learn from me, for I am gentle and humble in heart, and you will find rest for your souls. For my yoke is easy and my burden is light." I really had no real revelation of what it meant to be CHOSEN by God and the weight that it carried and the Authority it came with in the Spiritual realm but I was definitely going to find out. The word declares that many are called but FEW ARE CHOSEN!!!

Prophets are born prophets despite what many may believe. I kept asking God who AM I? What did you call me to do? What are my spiritual gifts? God I just feel like I'm all over the place. I often found myself running not knowing my calling wasn't just going to go anywhere. I remember telling God like I just want to love you, worship you and grow in your word that's it. I don't want to be responsible for people. I don't even like your children like that honestly cause people always have something to say. God and you know how my mouth is set up. I really want to read them their rights (tell them about themselves). Please get somebody else to do it! I gave God all these excuses like what if I mess up, what if I get something wrong , God why me?

He said stop asking why me. I am God and I know what's best for you. I knew you before I placed you in your mother's womb. He said I called you to this, I chose you for this, you can handle this. I said well what kind of Prophet am I then God and he took me right in the book Of Jeremiah and I began to read and learn more about his time as a prophet. He told Jeremiah "Before I formed thee in the belly I knew thee; and before thou camest forth out of the womb I sanctified thee, and I ordained thee a prophet unto the nations. Jeremiah went on to tell the Lord how he was just a child and how he couldn't speak. God went on to tell him not to say I am a child for he shall go to all that he shall send him to and whatever he commands him to speak he must speak it. God went on to tell him "Do not be afraid of their faces: for I am with thee to deliver thee, saith the Lord." Then he touched Jeremiah's mouth and said unto him Behold I have put my words in thy mouth. He says: "See I have this day set thee over the nations and over the kingdoms, to root out, and to pull down, and to destroy, and to throw down, to build, and to plant.

It was A lot to take in but as I often say I said well God I don't understand you but I trust you and you know what's best for my life. As I continued to go through life it made sense why my life was everything but normal, whatever "normal" means. By this I mean I couldn't do certain things and go to certain places but others could and they wouldn't have any sense of conviction. I'm like what's wrong with me? Everyone loved me when I was depressed and full of despair but when I was filled with the HOLY SPIRIT people didn't know how to take me and told me I was too deep, it doesn't take all that and it's not that serious. At first, it made me just kind of run from God cause God if this is really your doing shouldn't it be different but after learning more about the word of God I learned many like the idea of God but not really the TRUE POWER that comes with living a life in the spirit and living a life in a posture of PRAISE, WORSHIP, PRAYER, AND FASTED before God (life of consecration before God). Many people like the idea of me but can't handle what comes with the calling on my life. This has caused others to speak ill of me instead of getting to know me for themselves. Make no mistake, I'm far from perfect. In fact I messed up so many times that I'm like God I'm just checking in to make sure you didn't change your mind about lil ole me.

Many people walked away from me because of the calling on my life but I know God has fully equipped me and he told me for this next season he is sending me help. I only need to trust and obey! He told me he will uphold me with his righteous right hand! That was all I needed to know. As the word declares "IF GOD BE FOR ME THEN WHO CAN BE AGAINST ME" Here I am fully submitted and trusting God to use me as he sees fit. He knows what's best for me. My favorite scripture easily became Jeremiah 29:11 For I know the plans I have for you, plans to prosper you and not harm you, plans to give you a hope and a future. This became my favorite scripture because there was a time when the enemy tried to make me believe that I would be better off dead and everyone would be happy. He used to try to convince me to just kill myself and that if I did I wouldn't have to suffer anymore. I now know that's a life from the pits of hell. TO GOD BE GLORY! I'M STILL STANDING, I'M STILL ALIVE!

Chapter 5

Forgiving Myself and others

For a long time, I struggled with forgiving myself but it was much easier to forgive others. It was hard to forgive myself for things that I had done such as the abortion, gossipping, and even for the things that I allowed to happen to me out of ignorance or just plain stupidity… like I knew better BUT GOD! Somebody said it like this: "he does not treat us as our sin deserves." There were periods in my life that I have had some deep wounds that I now know and understand that it was only by the grace of God and literally being transformed by the renewing of my mind that I was able to forgive some situations as the wounds sometimes seemed as if they would never heal, I mean they cut me DEEP DEEP.

It has not always been easy to forgive. In fact I'll take it a step further and say it was in fact a struggle at a certain point in my life. I would say God but you don't understand what they did, like they really have me messed up on so many different levels. I was quickly reminded that Jesus who had no sin got on the cross who was crucified and he paid the ultimate price, he paid a price that I could never afford to pay.

As I began to grow in my relationship with my heavenly Father, I have to admit that there were a lot of things that I didn't necessarily understand or even agree with but I do know that his word is true and how I feel does not move God. He is more concerned with my heart's posture and whether or not I will obey even when it's hard, even when people despitefully use me and plan and plot all manners of evil towards me. I just want to encourage someone that if you have asked God for forgiveness and have repented meaning you have turned away from that sin then you have to trust and believe that he is faithful to forgive you and forget that sin (no memory of it). In the same manner we cannot expect that we can ask God for forgiveness and walk around here not forgiving others. In fact, God tells us very specifically Matthew 6:14–15 AMP version: "For if you forgive others their trespasses [their reckless and willful sins], your heavenly Father will also forgive you. But if you do not forgive others [nurturing your hurt and anger with the result that it interferes with your relationship with God], then your Father will not forgive your trespasses."

Chapter 6

Witchcraft (Spiritual Wickedness in High Places)

I was completely blind to the spiritual wickedness in high places. It would be later in my walk that I would come to learn more about the workings of the enemy in the churches and those who say God God but they are as far from him as the east is the west. I was introduced to witchcraft unbeknownst to me when I was parting ways with my job as a supervisor of a very prominent healthcare company in my hometown and all across VA and beyond. I left this job on a mission to focus on a degree program and pursue a business opportunity. That failed, I learned that was not a part of his plan for my life.

This woman whom I met on an elevator at a previous job now also worked under me just not as my direct report. If you know anything about me you know I love music, specifically praise and worship. I was created to PRAISE!! Hallelujah is the highest praise!

It was my first day on the new job and the building that our job was in was located inside a multiple-business complex. We both got in the elevator and she spoke and gave her name and I shared mine as well. I shared it was my first day and asked if she could tell me where Sutherland Healthcare Solutions was. She was glad to help me as that's where she was also headed. This was a job where we did PDM (provider data management) amongst other tasks depending on the workload. We were able to listen to music as we worked as this specific role did not require us to be on the phones. It was perfect for me because again when I'm listening to my praise and worship I feel like nothing else matters. I get an excitement and that unspeakable joy and perfect peace.

I'm not sure how much time had passed but one day she asked me what kind of music I was listening to and I told her and at this particular it was one of Tasha Cobbs new albums "GRACE" and she advised that she hadn't heard of it and told me thank you for sharing it with her as she was going through a time of bereavement, someone in her family had recently passed away. That was pretty much the extent of our relationship. Talking about God and sharing music with one another. I stayed at this job for about 3 yrs and then I applied for a job at the healthcare company previously mentioned and they actually wanted to bring me on as a supervisor instead and I quickly accepted the offer. This was a pay increase of $10+, I definitely didn't know what to expect but I trusted God for my next level and moved forward with accepting the offer.

I was one of three supervisors hired and I would say me and the other 2 young ladies had a pretty decent working relationship as we helped one another to effectively manage all teams individually and collectively. Our favorite lunch spots when we all went together was this hibachi place called SUMO, that was our escape from the craziness of the claims world and managing our teams. If my memory serves me correctly I had about 15-20 people that reported directly to me.

Many people from my previous company ended up leaving and also coming to this company under the same claims dept that I was hired at as the TC (team coordinator or supervisor). We had to go through extensive training to learn the different claim types to include PCP, Lab, DME, Outpatient and AmbSurgery just to name a few. What I respected about this company was that they made the supervisors go through the training as well as the associates. My only suggestion would have been to bring the supervisors on earlier than the team. I felt as if our training should have been separate but the company was of the mindset that this would be a good way for us to keep an eye on our teams, get to know them and see who may struggle and who would catch on quickly.

I quickly learned that while financially I was doing pretty well for myself I was not fulfilled and satisfied doing this job. Supervising was cool but much like other things of course it came with pros and cons. There were days I simply wanted to just be able to come in and do my own work and go home. As a supervisor that was not an option. Outside of the supervisor aspect of this position, we received a new director and baby, it was just something about her that I knew her spirit was not right. I'm all about respecting my elders and leadership but I'm of the thought I'm grown and if I don't talk to you crazy don't talk to me crazy.

We had A VP that also talked to us in a belittling way. I used to sit in those meetings zoned out because I really didn't understand the nastiness and who they thought they were talking to whew chile. Anyhow, I knew I had two options at this point. I was either going to resign and possibly be able to work at this company again later if needed or I was going to get fired for having to respectfully read them their rights i.e tell them about themselves in a nice nasty way.

When I left this position it was September of 2018. I had a plan but it clearly wasn't God's plan because while I just knew this was what God wanted I eventually found myself not following through and not being fulfilled again. When I was leaving this lady previously mentioned gave me some sort of peace of clay with a scripture also. I didn't really see the significance so I really didn't pay it much attention. She said "I want you to have this." Again, they say if you want a good laugh tell God your plans. I made the choice to move back with my parents by choice not force because I was working with this organization that helped to repair credit and also taught financial literacy. I saw the business opportunity, the option to fix my own credit and help others while getting paid. It was a no brainer for me to sign me up right? Well so I thought. I had plans to go back to my parents house where I could pay less and save up for a house.

I clearly saw very shortly after leaving my job that things were not going according to how I saw them and really felt like I had probably just made a big mistake, one which I wasn't going to be able to undo. I had let my job go, so I didn't renew my lease at my old apartment at this time. I was doing well financially initially while trying to grow with the business opportunity which I felt like initially was going to put me in position to purchase my first home and help others to do the same. I have to be honest in saying there were times where I didn't feel like praising and worshipping and reading the word which I now know is exactly how the enemy was able to trick me. The word lets us know we are to continually seek him. We are to pray without ceasing. 1 Peter 5:8 Declares be sober, be vigilant, because your adversary the devil walketh about as a roaring lion, seeking whom he may devour. I also did not have a lifestyle of praying and fasting so I was battling things in the spirit and was not properly equipped to withstand it. I didn't notice at first and was not aware of a monitoring spirit but the Holy Spirit later revealed to me that's exactly what the lady who gave me that piece of clay as a parting gift possessed.

She told me about my future before I fully knew what God was going to do in and through my life. The Holy Spirit instructed me to get the clay and throw everything away as it was a means to track and trace me in the spirit and cause a demonic delay in my life. She would always tell me she couldn't wait for me to finish my book. She was going to buy 20 copies and give them away. I can now look and laugh but when all of this was revealed I was like wayment now God you said what? She recently reached out to me inquiring about my marriage and of course access was denied. I don't play with demons. Find somebody else to do it!

Now this next person that did witchcraft on me hit differently because she was supposed to be my "best friend". Our friendship started at this place called TRG customer solutions. It was somewhere late in 2008, early 2009 if my memory serves me correct. Now looking back I now know it was a trauma bond and not something authentic or pure sent from God. I still never expected she would ultimately try to take my life. To be honest I don't even recall how we became close. I know we started hanging out amongst some other friends that I won't name. We would often talk about where we were and how we wanted to get serious about our futures because we both felt like working a standard 9-5 was not it. No shade to anyone but I just always knew God had more for me. I was never fulfilled in any job. I would constantly think about the book I felt like I was supposed to write. I would go up in praise trying to contain it so no one would think I was crazy and plus I was on someone else's clock. The best way to describe it was I often found myself there but not there if that makes sense. I would go on to have my first child, my beautiful daughter and almost 2 years later my handsome son. She always showed up when no one else would and made it seem as if she was the only one there for me but the whole time it was never genuine and the holy spirit later revealed she actually hated my very guts. She was an "Angel of Light" The bible tells us that the Devil "disguises himself as an angel of light." 2 Corinthians 11:14-15

Can you imagine how sick that is to have someone that close to you that doesn't even like you. I regarded this girl as a sister and she was around to help assist me with a few of my daughter's sleepovers. I remember her telling me one year this my last year helping you with these sleepovers with what I now know was a sense of agitation because people can only pretend for so long. We were "friends" for several years and I didn't even know she had a voice and she really could sing. One year I asked her to sing happy birthday to me because I loved music and why not. I love music, that's just how God equipped me. So she did but what she said on the recording before singing happy birthday was a red flag but with an undertone of joking. We have to be mindful that if we pay attention people will not always tell you how they feel about you but they will certainly show you. She sang happy birthday but her introduction was "Happy bday little worrisome girl." Still thinking nothing of it. I just brushed it off as she was playing and moved on about my day. She was one of the many I assisted in getting in the door at the second healthcare company I mentioned previously. As A TC I had direct access to HR and they would often take resumes from the supervisors if we had people that we thought might be a good fit. So naturally when she gave me her resume I passed it on to HR and she received the call. I'll never take God's glory but I was just a vessel used in helping her get in the door.

Her being my "bestfriend" I had insight from the associate's point of view. She would often tell me what happened in training as she started a few classes behind my class. Oftentimes on the phone our conversations consisted of me dealing with my children's father cause I couldn't understand for the life of me why I was going through what I was going through like what did I ever do to deserve this? When she would complain about work and the teams she would often say "people want to come in here and manage but can't even manage their lives at home and it didn't really hit me until after the fact she was talking about me.. We fell out a few times but we reconnected. I just knew it was God. It was cool at first we talked about God and just tried to elevate despite what our situations looked like in front of us. This was short lived. I always sensed something was off but I couldn't put my hand on it. My mom was usually very good about telling us about people who were our friends and those who weren't. I now know it was God putting a check in my spirit but if we aren't careful we allow the love we have for others to literally blind us in the spirit.

God had been warning me all along but I just was not getting it. I always believed that one day God would fix my situation but because I had someone who was pretending in my face and was sent as a destiny destroyer I was delayed. She always said to me "you sure God said that cause that's not what I'm getting when I would share something with her." It would cause me to doubt cause I believed spiritually she knew more and was wiser than me in the things of God. It almost made me want to stop pursuing God cause I knew I wasn't a liar but I began to get confused like God I don't understand cause I don't proclaim to be the most holiest but I know I worship and praise you in spirit and truth. This cycle continued for what seemed like forever. She used to call me lele, someone else started that nickname. As I started to slowly but surely distance myself little by little I guess she could feel it in the spirit. She quickly conjured up a lie and a plan with her family to tell me God said she had to let me go.

Prior to doing this she told me she was going to consecrate herself to seek God for something. I knew in my spirit it was in regards to me. She told me she wouldn't be talking on the phone etc., At this time I can say I had never really fasted forreal forreal so I let her be. After she came off her fast, it was really what she said that got to me and immediately I got a sunken feeling in my stomach. She went on to say " I have to talk to you, it's a lot but I don't want to have this conversation on the phone.. She said this is a conversation that we shouldn't have over the phone. I initially agreed but something just felt so off I can't explain it. I let her know while I was willing to talk, it had to be done over the phone because my schedule really didn't permit me to meet with her, which was the truth and I certainly wasn't going to go out of my way since I got a check in my spirit about the whole thing anyway.

She didn't like that response but went on ahead and told me she has to let me go because God said I was a distraction and he is taking her somewhere that I can't go. She went on to say she asked God for confirmation and her mom said it was me that God told her to let go and her aunt said I was draining her. She said her aunt said I was like a clogged drain or something like that and that nothing could get through. Completely taken back I said okay I respect that. It didn't make sense to me but she said God said so I had to respect it. I don't want to be in trouble with God, who was I to question God or have her disobey God.

I was hurt. I talked to my mom about it and I mean it was hard cause me and her talked a lot so I felt kind of lost…My mom said Shalil, I knew from when I had you that you've always been a special child and very blessed by God. At this moment I heard what she said but it didn't make sense because why would God allow this kind of heartbreak when I was learning how to grow closer to him with her help so I thought. My mom said I think she was jealous of you. Now I am never the one to say someone is jealous of me because it's just never been that serious to me. We are supposed to walk around like we are that girl insecurities and all, not prideful though just have a Godly confidence. I'm like mom this girl can sing, like blow why would she be jealous of little ole me..? I am a firm believer that what God has for me is for me and what God has for someone else is for them. We have to be very careful not to covet the gifts of others. I always just knew I loved being in a place of worship before God, I never knew he gave me a

GIFT OF PRAISE! By and by!

Anyways…I took it one day at a time healing and questioning God about what I did so bad that you had to tell her to cut off the relationship? Though it hurt me, it blessed me and it caused me to search out and seek God like I had never before. As much as I was hurt, God was still God and for me I knew there was no life apart from God.I knew that just because a person left my life or I left a church that didn't mean God left me. Pastors please stop telling this lie from the pits of hell. God is not going to punish you when your season is up at a church that's demonic to suggest that.

Like three weeks after telling me God told her to cut me off she texts me and sends me a song that she wrote and recorded. I've never been a hater and always gave props where they were due. So naturally, I told her I liked it and left it there. Months go by. I'm minding my business and my mom, my daughter, my baby sis, my niece and my dad take a day trip to Ocean City, MD for his birthday. As we are getting ready to prepare to come back home I get a text from her. Before I got this text from her my daily devotion had just come in letting me know that someone was going to try to come back in my life. Minutes later I got a text from her and she asked me if she could call me. I was reluctant and told her I was in the car she could but I couldn't really talk.

She went on to tell me how her ex and her son's Father recently got married. In my mind I'm like okayyyy…and that has SOMETHING to do with me because????. Of course I didn't say that though God is yet still working on me. I let her vent then she was like I don't want you to feel like I'm just calling you to vent. However, that is in fact what she was doing. It became very apparent the things she was accusing me of she was actually doing to me. I later learned she thought that by leaving me when she knew I felt like I needed her the most she would break my spirit. God instead healed me and taught me to really lean and depend on him and strengthened my ability to seek him out for myself.

She kept trying to come back around but again I'm like I don't think that's a good idea because you said God said to let me go right?. She never would really address that. One day she asked me to go eat with her. I was very reluctant but went anyway. I was very quiet. She began to say as we were riding in the car "this feels awkward doesn't it… like when you get back with someone without any explanation." I just maintained nah I'm good, I'm just listening. She wanted to start doing bible studies together and stuff and I was like nah I'm okay I'm taking this journey alone for now and plus my mom told me "Shalil, be careful with her that was all my mom said."

I later had strabismus surgery which if you're not aware of what that is, it's is a surgery where if you have lazy eyes they surgically try to make them function like they should. I came home from surgery and was made aware that my eyes would be red for weeks to come. She came and checked on me at my parent's house. My daughter mostly cared for me and made sure I took my medicine on time etc., Somehow I ended up feeling sick and found I had pneumonia after the surgery. She got wind of me having surgery and she brought me some type of orange pills in a ziploc bag. She informed me that they were "vitamin C pills" and they helped her when she wasn't feeling well and had pneumonia. I took probably one or two and for some reason never took anymore. I now know it was God. She would ask me, "Did you take your pill today? I'm like nah and she's like if you want to get better you need to take those. I didn't think much of it but just didn't keep taking them. Time goes on and I get a second and third confirmation that I need to let the relationship go by way of a preached word and by a male friend of mine (well ex-friend). He is not a believer but he said Shalil I don't know much about God but I don't know anyone else is as serious about their walk as you at this age, that girl tried to break you, she couldn't have been your friend.

I prayed to God for a strategy and a way to let her know that I was parting ways. Though she tried to break me I know I didn't need to try to get even. It wasn't right or even in my heart or mind to do. He says vengeance is mine sayeth The Lord, I will repay. I formulated a text to say I appreciate her and who she had been to me but I know we are going in different directions. She sent a very nasty text. I read it and kept moving about my day. That was the last I heard from her until the Holy Spirit had me send a message of warning to her to tell her to repent. It was a strong message of warning. It was so heavy that I had such a heavy feeling until I released that word. She told me that was not from God and asked me to never text her again. The dream I had before the Holy Spirit led me in scripture to send her that text scared the life out of me. It's a dream I'll never forget as long as I live. I literally saw a pool of blood. I said Lord what's going on, what are you showing me. That's when he led me in his word to send her the text. She knew at this moment she had been found out and she no longer was disguised as a witch and a worker of the kingdom of darkness but that I now knew!

This is the text the Holy Spirit told me to send to her: REPENT Turn away from your wicked ways! He says you can run but you cannot hide! Every man will have his day!

"But every one shall die for his own iniquity: every man that eateth the sour grape, his teeth shall be set on edge." Jeremiah 31:30

"For God shall bring every work into judgment, with every secret thing, whether it be good, or whether it be evil." Ecclesiates 12:14

But I say unto you, That every idle word that men shall speak, they shall give an account thereof in the day of judgment."

Matthew 12:36 If my people who are called by my name will humble themselves and pray and seek my face, and turn from their wicked ways, then I will hear from heaven, and I will forgive their sins and heal their land."

She went on to say that was not from God as he does not contradict himself and it was okay to call my God son but other than that please stop texting her. I went on to let her know I won't argue as this was from God.. I had a heaviness until I released that word. I told her she was ABSOLUTELY RIGHT God does not contradict himself but as humans we can. I told her to be blessed and kiss my God baby for me. I was led to cut all ties and have never heard from her again.

I would later go on a fast and the Holy Spirit revealed so much more. He informed me that he had me trying to warn me but I wouldn't listen. I had too much clutter to hear clearly. He went on to say throw those pills and soap away that she gave me (it was a bar of soap and the pills previously mentioned.) He said she performed witchcraft on you. The Holy Spirit went on to inform me that soap caused that very dark mark on your face that won't go away and she was literally feeding you to your death with those pills. That is why she would call daily asking if you had taken your pill today. He said they were calculating your death and planning and plotting your death and burial. He said they were going to march into your service and stand over your dead body as if nothing ever happened but I wouldn't let it be so.

She had also gotten her license to do nails (or so I think). I came to find out she was a big liar even though we both would often talk about how much we disliked liars. She would always do her nails and me personally I always gave props where they were due. I asked her to do my nails and toes a few times and I would later find that my nails specifically, would break in such a way that didn't make any kind of sense. I knew something was off but couldn't put my hand on it. The Holy Spirit also revealed this was her doing, through witchcraft.

Prior to this being revealed I had also recently bought some hair oil from her sister and it was the craziest thing that happened. I used it once and one day I saw some sort of spark come from this bottle which I thought was strange. The Holy Spirit also said get that out of your house now. I was floored, like talking about weeping. It was then I knew she really hated me BUT GOD! I'll be honest once God revealed this to me I failed the test cause I really wanted to respond in my flesh cause like how dare she do this to me. After getting it off my chest I eventually let it go and asked God to heal me every time I was reminded of the offense I forgave again just to ensure I didn't give the enemy any legal rights or access to me through unforgiveness in my heart or bitterness in my heart.

Many people thought I was crazy. My kid's father even tried to tell the judge when we went to court for a custody visitation matter that the kids needed to be taken away because I had lost my mind and even some of my own family members said the same thing. I know it sounded crazy but I knew I wasn't a fiction story teller and would never intentionally lie to anyone. I'll be the first to say in my walk I have leaned to my own understanding before but I was no liar. I always asked God to allow me to have a pure heart before him and if I said something wrong to anyone convict me and I surely will apologize and repent.

This was not one of those cases and the Holy Spirit confirmed it on another fast because I said God I want to know that I know that I wasn't wrong concerning what I heard you tell me. God confirmed and not only that told me to stop questioning what I heard him say. He said to me I will uphold you with my righteous right hand. He said I walk and I talk with you. I tell you that you are my own. He told me I am sending help your way. He said I allowed it. I also allowed people to think you lost your mind.

He said I have assigned you to dark places to fight wickedness in high places. HE SAID DON'T BE AFRAID OF THEM IN THEIR FACE. He said you only need to trust and obey.

He said I will send confusion to your enemies. Joshua 10:10-11 The Lord threw them into confusion before Israel, so Joshua and the Israelites defeated them completely at Gibeon. Israel pursued them along the road going up to

Beth Horon and cut them down all the way to Azekah and Makkedah. As they fled before Israel on the road down from Beth Horon to Azekah, the LORD hurled large hailstones down on them, and more of them died from the hail then were killed by the swords of the israelites.

Chapter 7

I was afflicted -he healed my body

I was born to my parents as Shalil Pooser and though they would often tell me Shalil, you are precious to God it was really hard for me to believe because I would look at my sisters and feel like God how come I'm the only one with lazy eyes and how come I'm the only one with bad acne that seems to not get better no matter what. It would come several years later that I would come to understand that God didn't love me any less and that he also did not make any mistakes when he made me. His word tells me that I am fearfully and wonderfully made. He knows me by name. He says I am more precious than rubies. He says he knew me before he placed me in my mother's womb. He said he knew the plans he has for me, plans to prosper me and not to harm me. Plans to give me a hope and a future. Jeremiah 29:11 quickly became my favorite scripture because for so long I would say to myself this can't be life. Why am I here God? Do you really have a plan for my life? My battle with acne got better but I'm believing in God for total victory. People who have never suffered with acne could never imagine the devastation and just the desire to just wake up with clear skin.I tried several over the counter medicines and different dermatologists but nothing seemed to work. This coupled with blemishes I just felt a mess but in all this God taught me how to love me unconditionally. He reminded me he is after the heart of man but he is also concerned with those things that concern me. I had to also take accountability and realize I needed to have a better diet to help aid in bettering my skin.

from hopeless TO VICTORIOUS

Chapter 8

My Knight and Shining Armor

This evening September 15th 2023 I was out with my children doing gig work specifically for a company called go puff. This was actually my first day testing this app out and to my surprise would be the day that would change my life forever. This was an order to Papa John in Norfolk, VA on 21st. He was working his part time job also. The app began to give me instructions letting me know this was an order that would require age verification and proper identification I.e a valid driver's license or identification card. Again this was my very first order so I wanted to ensure I did a great job. Initially I thought the app was experiencing a glitch or malfunctioning because it was taking me to papa johns and not someone's actual residence. As I circled to find a parking spot this man I now know as my husband began to walk outside and ask if I was with go puff because he placed an order. I advised I was and as the app began to take me through the prompts it let me know that I could not deliver this vape to him at this place of business. I asked him to give me a few seconds so I can assure I'm not missing something or mistaking what I feel like the app is requesting of me.I walked back to my car and called their customer service team to see what the issue was and why I could not deliver this vape. They explained and I felt really bad because it was my first order and of course this man wanted this vape I assumed. I got out of the car and asked my daughter to walk with me to let him know cause I didn't know this man from a can of paint and just wanted to be on the safe side.. she was something like my bodyguard lol not really but really. Anyhow we proceeded to inform him of the news and to my surprise he took the news exceptionally well. Though it wasn't my fault, I apologized for the inconvenience and let him know that per the app I was instructed to return the order to the facility.

Once I knew the coast was clear I told my daughter she can go ahead and go back in the car with her brother he was knocked out in the back seat. I was still in a very good view of them in the car. He began to smile at me and asked if he could call me sometimes. I looked over at my daughter as she was looking at me but also not able to hear our conversation. He told me his name was and said he just wanted to talk to me. He didn't want any problems with my bodyguard.. I.e my daughter lol. I told him both of my children are just protective over their mother. He proceeded to tell me I had a beautiful smile and he appreciated how I handled this exchange as I went above and beyond because most people would have just said you can't have the order and just left. We chopped it up for a few mins and he learned my name and also shared with me that he had a son with a name similar to mine. I thought that was cute. I gave him my number and we talked and began to come to know one another better.

When I met him I was fully clothed and had on this long green coat. He told me that I looked nice even though I felt like I looked a mess and I had some old braids. I had just come back from A work trip when I was employed with AAA as A PIP Adjuster. In my mind I'm like sir, I look like a good mess. I'm simply just trying to make ends meet as a single mother.

We went on to talk, we exchanged pictures and continued to get to know one another. Things began to blossom and move along pretty quick. Sometimes he would ask to ride with me when I did orders because he didn't want me out there by myself. I was very appreciative of it but I just always had this knowing that God has always protected and watched over me. I had wisdom to know that I needed to always be watchful and mindful where I plant my feet and go but again I just had this inner knowing that God got me and that this was temporary, this place of poverty and just barely making it was not my forever and it would not always be like this.

For any parents doing what it takes to get the job done I commend you it's not easy but God is yet still working that situation out for you even now. Declare that over your life and know that he is able to do exceedingly abundantly more than you can ask or think. But as it is written: eyes have not seen, nor ear heard, nor have it entered into the heart of man the things which God has prepared for those who love him. I'm talking about My God, Big God not the little one. PRAISE BREAK!!! Anywho….

I found myself falling into sin and let him know I'm sorry but I can't do this like you cool and all but I have to answer to God. You're not my husband yet and he was okay with it. He asked me to come to church with me after only like a week and because I attend a small church I was a little uneasy about it because I'm like well I don't want to deny you to come to church on the one hand but on the other my kids would be with me and I never played about my kids like that and introducing them to people before I knew really where it was going. I told him how I felt in regards to it and he understood but not really because in his mind he just wanted to go to church. As I went to church the next Sunday as I was sitting in worship I got convicted. It hit me like a ton of bricks. I'm like Lord, what is it? The Holy Spirit began to tell me Shalil, it's not about you, this is much bigger than you. Move yourself out of the way.

I talked to "my brothers" about it after service and let them know about the situation. They began to say yeah sis not many men want to even come to church nowadays so don't deny him that opportunity just make sure he knows where you stand with the situation so there is no confusion. My brother went on to say sis you don't know what may be released that he needs. I called him after church and apologized and repented to God for denying him the opportunity to come to church with me. This was a lesson for me because while I thought it was wise to protect my children by waiting to let him attend with us, God already knew the plan he had for our lives even before he allowed us to meet. He reminded me that it is not by mistake that you were sent as his delivery driver and he couldn't get the vape. I was simply using you as a vessel.

It became very apparent after some short time that this man was not going to leave my side and he trusted the God in me. He said he knew he felt something special from our first encounter and the way I handled his situation. It didn't take us very long to know that we wanted to spend the rest of our lives together. We went to our "pastor" at the time and told her that we wanted to get married and wanted to first receive marriage counseling. She said she already knew what was up before I even told her. I loved her real bad. We began marriage counseling and we learned a lot that would surely become a test and trial in our marriage but God. This was around November and once we completed marriage counseling we set a date for Feb 2, 2024. Of course when we shared the news there were those who were in support of it and asked if I had prayed about it first… then there were those who weren't of course. Many asked what the rush was and my answer to that was that it really was no rush but that we both loved one another and I knew it was A God thing. He had his own relationship with God and gained so much wisdom over the years but much like anyone else needed help with his walk and never pretended to be someone he wasn't, that's what I loved and respected about him. I not only loved him but I knew I was in love with him. I was reminded that God is not impressed by the outward appearance of a man and his possessions as the world is but God is concerned with the heart of man. He truly has a heart of Gold and I can't speak to other women's experience before me but I knew that he loved me.

In the words of Lyfe Jennings when you got someone good you hold onto them. Still no engagement at this point but I knew it was coming just not how or when. I did throw him lil hints of how I wanted it but I didn't know if he was even paying attention to those things. I wanted someone to be able to capture the moment which happened. I gave him this list of things and he probably was like girl boo in his mind but I thank God he has a mind of his own and he's not consumed by the things that others are. It was intimate and perfect to me. He's so romantic and I love that about him. He's not perfect but neither am I clearly and I thank God for keeping me and keeping us anyhow.

Chapter 9

Miscarriage

I learned even prior to completing marriage counseling I was pregnant. I sat myself down. (Wasn't sharing God's word with others)...I didn't want to be a hypocrite but even in this I was reminded that God is not the accuser of brethren that's satan and his minions. I thought about what everyone was going to say but realized there was no way I was getting an abortion I did the sin and I had already told God I would never get another abortion. I repented and God had forgiven me and through it in the sea of forgetfulness. Me and my husband, fiance' at this time vowed to abstain from sex until we actually got married and said I do. It was met with a little resistance at first but I'm so glad that he understood when I said while I love you, I love God more and I'm not going to be found guilty of playing with God especially when I know better. I never want to abuse his grace and mercy over my life. We got married on February 2nd 2024 and it was soooo beautiful, small and intimate.

My brother in law was having a birthday celebration the next day as his birthday was the same day as our wedding day. Even though I wasn't feeling the best, me and my husband wanted to support and attended his birthday dinner.. Unbeknownst to me I was in fact beginning to miscarry. I had a doctor's appointment at about what should have been 10 weeks pregnant for me. They felt like something was wrong and the baby was not growing on schedule because the baby was still measuring at about 6 weeks. I immediately grew concerned but trusted God and said God I don't understand but I trust you. Back to us being at my brother in law's bday dinner. I began to feel something wet.. Now mind you, they weren't 100% sure that I would miscarry but knew it was a high possibility because our baby was not growing on schedule but at the time of my last visit our baby still had a heart beat. As I begin to eat and chat with my sister and one of her friends, blood starts flowing from me. I was so embarrassed and quickly motioned for my husband that we had to leave and go to the emergency room.

We quickly notified a few people so no one would worry why we left in such a rush and then headed for the car. My husband walked around to let me in the car and put something on the seat so I wouldn't stain it. TMI but as you can imagine blood continued to flow from me while enroute to the emergency room. We went to Sentara Princess Anne where my husband walked me to the front and proceeded to go and park the car. As I walked in I felt blood flowing down my legs. I quickly went to the counter to let them know I am losing a lot of blood and I am pregnant. I don't feel like they moved with enough urgency for me so I reminded them I AM PREGNANT. I had an urge to go to the bathroom and when I did I felt a big gush and that is when I passed a few blood clots. It happened so fast that they fell to the floor before I could fully pull my pants down and relieve the need to urinate. I was stuck and shocked. I went to the door of this private bathroom to motion for my husband and a nurse. I didn't know what to do. She rolled a wheelchair to the door and they quickly rolled me to the back after getting all my vital information from my husband. They rolled me to the back and got me into a room. My husband helped me to get undressed and remove the saturated pants I had on. I knew at this point our precious baby was no more. They rushed around me trying to get the bleeding to stop and asked if I was anemic which I informed them I wasn't and if I'm not mistaken they confirmed through blood work. They were finally able to stop the bleeding temporarily. They gave me something to speed up the process of removing the remains of what would not pass on its own so I would not get an infection.

They informed me it could happen very quickly or it could be a slow process. It was literally just a waiting game. Mind you I had a doctor's appointment a few days before we got married so I was essentially starting to miscarry on our wedding day. It was a bittersweet day. This was pain that I wouldn't wish on anyone. I had to go back to the hospital 2 more times before it was all said and done. I still don't understand but again I trust that God knows best and he can see what I can't. I believe that he will give us double for our trouble in his divine timing. It was later revealed that many placed a curse on our marriage and even preyed against my womb and our unborn child. God revealed who had a hand in what but I've already forgiven them and pray that God will have mercy on them. I learned some time ago though, some offenses cut deep, especially from those you view as family and friends forgive quickly and release people in the freedom of your forgiveness. God knows how to handle your enemies way better than you ever can. Let God be God and don't block your blessings trying to repay evil for evil. Nothing gets by God. Bless your enemies and those that despitefully use you. When God says to leave and remove yourself, remove yourself and cut ties. I don't care who it is. God sees and knows the hearts of everyone and he loves you too much to leave you where you were.

God bless you and thank you for reading!

ATTACHED YOU'LL FIND A COPY OF MY POEM WHERE I OPEN ABOUT MY BATTLE WITH DEPRESSION EVEN AS A BELIEVER. I NOW KNOW THAT I HAVE THE POWER OVER THE ENEMY! I INCLUDED THIS AS IS WAS APART OF MY JOURNEY FROM WHERE GOD HAS BROUGHT ME TO WHERE HE'S TAKING ME AND HOW HE HAS CHANGED MY MIND!

I AM GOING TO RUN ON AND SEE WHAT THE END IS LIKE!

JOHN 13:7 "YOU DON'T UNDERSTAND NOW WHAT I'M DOING BUT IT WILL BE CLEAR ENOUGH TO YOU LATER."

POEM: "AWAKEN" Originally written in 2017 Prophetic Poem

Full of so much hurt and pain,
Oftentimes it seems like a game.
In the Black community, it's not real,
We stay quiet—no one wants to know how we feel.

It's a silent killer, we don't broadcast,
And even when we're struggling, we wear a mask.
Some can't take it, feel they have no choice,
Taking their life, the only way to voice.

It's a battle, too ashamed to speak,
Made to believe it's not real, not weak.
But I'm here to tell you, my sister or brother,
I know how you feel, like no one can understand another.

I could talk for days, still not cover it all,
The depths of this pain, the silent call.
But today I'm speaking out to heal,
To help my sisters and brothers feel.

To those who've never felt depression's grip,
It seems like you're crazy, slipping from your grip.
But what you feel is so real and deep,
You just want your mind to rest and sleep.

Mind racing, decisions weighing,
Should I stay or should I go, staying?
All I think of is Taniyah and Terrance,
My babies, will they ever forgive me, is there a chance?

Tears streaming down, questioning if I can stay,
Mentally, wondering if I'm built to face another day.
It feels like those who love me laugh in my face,
Screaming inside, I try to wear a smile, but it's not in place.

from hopeless TO VICTORIOUS

Some days I leap from bed with praise,
Other days, I force myself through the haze.
All I want is sleep to take the pain away,
But it's temporary—just a trick of the enemy's sway.

The mind is his playground, I'm losing my fight,
He whispers lies in the dark of night.
Telling me no one cares, no one's near,
Convinces me it's over, that I'm nothing but fear.

I begin to question, was I a mistake?
Does God have a plan for me, or is that fake?
Why do I feel this way? What is this pain?
What did you create me to do, Lord? What's my gain?

Sleep is essential, but too much is a trap,
It distracts me from what's in store, from God's map.
I've accomplished much, overcome so much pain,
But this feeling grips tight, wants to remain.

Yet in the darkness, I hear a song,
God whispers to me, telling me I belong.
Music is therapy, it lifts my soul,
But when it ends, I'm alone, losing control.

God wakes me in the night with a call,
"Get up, my child, it's time to stand tall."
You've been sleeping long enough, let go of your fears,
You have a life to live, don't drown in your tears.

Shalil Forrest

There's love around you, family and friends,
But most of all, a God who'll never let go, never ends.
Fearfully and wonderfully made,
More than a conqueror, His promises won't fade.

At times, the bad outweighs the good,
And all I ask is, why must my walk be this tough?
I know you're shaping me, molding me for more,
But I still need your touch, to settle the war.

As selfish as it sounds, my mind goes there,
Sometimes I feel death would be a relief, a prayer.
I never imagined such pain as a child,
But here I stand, broken and wild.

You know He's able, yet I wonder if I'm the hold,
Is He waiting for me to see it's not about me, but the story told?
It's not about me, but His perfect will,
For every unbeliever to witness the power still.

I get it now, God, I understand,
Continue to lead me and take me by the hand.
There is purpose in my pain,
Help me hold on and make it through the rain.

I'm not living to die but to live again,
Depression is real, and that's where I've been.
So to my sisters and brothers, I'll say this loud,
I know it's hard, but together we'll be proud.

I know how you feel, I know your pain,
But you'll make it through, you'll rise again.

www.ingramcontent.com/pod-product-compliance
Lightning Source LLC
Chambersburg PA
CBHW070049230426
43661CB00005B/834